Components and Connections

Principles of Construction

Dedicated to my teachers Leen Hulsbos and Ruud Sackman

Maarten Meijs, Ulrich Knaack

Components and Connections
Principles of Construction

Birkhäuser
Basel · Boston · Berlin

We are grateful to Delft University of Technology for the financial support of this publication and to Ria Stein for her editorial guidance.
We acknowledge the help of Tillmann Klein, Jorien Diemel and Henk Mihl for their research, text advice and drawings.
The drawings where made by Jorrit Verduin, Vincent van Sabben, Farhan Alibux, Somayeh Chitchian and Jean-Paul Willemse.

Graphic design concept and cover: Oliver Kleinschmidt, Berlin
Layout and typesetting: MEDIEN PROFIS, Leipzig
Translation into English: Taalcentrum Vrije Universiteit, Amsterdam
Subject editing for the English edition: Jörn Frenzel, Berlin

This book is also available in a German edition:
ISBN 978-3-7643-8668-9

Library of Congress Control Number: 2009925662

Bibliographic information published by Die Deutsche Bibliothek
Die Deutsche Bibliothek lists this publication in the Deutsche
Nationalbibliografie; detailed bibliographic data is available in the
Internet at http://dnb.ddb.de.

© 2009 Birkhäuser Verlag AG
Basel · Boston · Berlin
P.O.Box 133, CH-4010 Basel, Switzerland
Part of Springer Science+Business Media
Printed on acid-free paper produced from chlorine-free pulp. TCF ∞
Printed in Germany

ISBN 978-3-7643-8668-9   *1007112240*

9 8 7 6 5 4 3 2 1

www.birkhauser.ch

CONTENTS

1 | Introduction

One may ask: why a book about components and connections? Numerous reference books provide explanations on individual building elements – such as slabs, roofs, beams, exterior and interior walls, doors, windows, balconies and stairs – and introduce standard details.

However, this book does not deal with the components individually, but sets out from the specific functions which the construction as a whole has to perform: it creates space, provides protection from the elements and external factors such as heat and cold, permits or prevents incident light and so on. These functions of the whole building essentially depend on the performance of individual building components. This book lines out how the components meet their requirements.

The book aims to provide an introduction into the field of building construction by merging its functional principles and requirements on one side with the structural options on the other. Thus, the reader will get a comprehensive overview enabling him or her to understand the individual principles and translate this knowledge into built constructions. Emphasis is on the relation of function and construction with regard to the respective components – rather than on isolated components as such.

Starting from the components the book will continue to elaborate on the various connections between them. A number of types of connections will be introduced, however, again not in terms of detailed solutions, but with a view to a superordinate system and according to specific classification criteria. Against this background, which effectively might be called a vocabulary and grammar of construction, various forms of constructions will be outlined. Based on the individual parts and their interconnection, this will enable readers to compose and deduce structural answers to structural questions: a process embedded in a holistic approach to a solution.

The appearance of a building and the composition of its individual components is guided by a large number of factors: aesthetics, trends, location and site-specific requirements, options for implementation, economy and legal frameworks. In any case two main criteria have to be met: stability and structural performance on one side, and permeability and/or tightness against external influences on the other. The chapter 'components' will explain what the individual building parts are composed of and elaborate on their technical performance. The chapter 'connections' introduces possible junctions in specific order: by their position between individual components, by their material or form. The last chapter 'building structure' eventually explains the three basic construction methods – solid construction, slab construction, skeleton construction – and outlines the interaction of primary and secondary or complementary structure.

Horizontal as well as vertical components form part of an entire construction and define the appearance of the building. Each of the components has its own build-up consisting of different layers varying in number. How and whether all requirements are being met depends on the type and dimension of the layers' material as well their position within the component, which is determined according to their function. This book lines out the underlying principles for this. Apart from enclosing a void, the components also have to provide access and views. They may take on entirely different forms and are ultimately subject to aesthetic preferences. The designer has an impact on the functionality of the construction as a whole by determining the materials, the dimension and composition of the components and their position. This process of optimisation forms an intrinsic part of design.

Making the function of components and connections the starting point of their consideration is beneficial for various reasons: firstly, components are subject to historic evolution. Over time, different components appeared and partly disappeared again as a result of a new state of arts or due to new developments in society – such as cost of building materials or labour. Environmental and energy-related aspects further changed type and shape of the components. This innovative process is in continuous flux, though the investment cost necessary for the development of new products is a hampering factor. A comprehensive schedule of individual components would inevitably soon be taken over by events and could only be a snapshot of a moment in time.

Contemporary architecture tends to blur the boundaries between individual components. While some literature still tries to pinpoint the boundary between wall and roof with a clear line and a 75° angle, this separation becomes entirely obsolete in the case of organically shaped 'blob' architecture: free-style architectural forms no longer allow for a sensible distinction between roof and wall.

The different forces onto walls and roofs like dead load or wind loads, rain or solar radiation precisely defy clear horizontal or vertical classification, but are rather gradual (1). Traditionally, certain materials or components are employed for horizontal or vertical constructions. However, there is no reason to believe that this form of use is compulsory and excludes innovative new interpretations.

This book essentially deals with the foundations of constructions and outlines their principles – last not least, to showcase the distinct characteristics of individual build-ups.

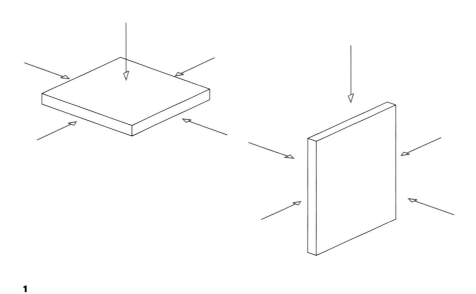

1

Impact of forces on surfaces
Both the horizontal and vertical surfaces are exposed to forces acting within the planes and perpendicular to them.

There are various examples for fluent transitions between roof and wall including the Sainsbury Centre in Norwich by Sir Norman Foster (2), Renzo Piano's Peek & Cloppenburg department store in Cologne (3) and the entry building by MVRDV to Hoge Veluwe nature reserve in the Netherlands (5).

The difference between an exterior wall and an interior partition may be ambiguous, too: though the wall between car park and house in a building with attached garage has to be thermally insulated, it does not have be weatherproof.

The structuring of information in this book will enable the reader – the future practitioner – to use his or her knowledge purposefully. In this context, emphasis is on the comprehension of principles allowing the designer to combine previous knowledge

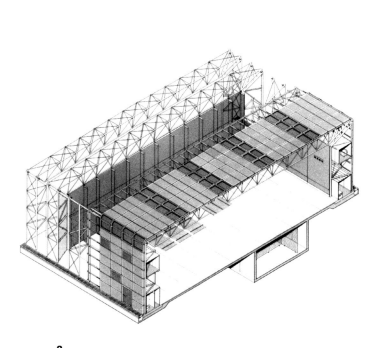

2

Sainsbury Centre for Visual Arts, Norwich, UK,
Sir Norman Foster, 1978
Roof and walls have the same constructive build-up.

3

Department store Peek & Cloppenburg, Cologne,
Renzo Piano, 2005
Wall and roof form a continuous shape.

with the ability to focus on the core issues in any future project. This new quality of knowledge will enable the reader to foster new solutions off the beaten track. This is important for two reasons: firstly, innovations are supposed to achieve more efficient solutions; secondly, there is a need to react to new and continuously changing circumstances. Although the compilation of knowledge is helpful en route to understanding the status quo, only structured knowledge supports an independent-minded approach to design. For the sake of one's own development and growth and society's capability to deal with pressing issues this would seem to be an absolute priority.

The classification scheme of this book takes a look at building construction from three directions generating a three-dimensional coordinate system as 'space of knowledge' (4). According to the specific axis it offers the opportunity for systematisation of knowledge. For example, this 'space of knowledge' can be subdivided into types of construction, thus distinguishing individual design principles. The same can be done with regard to materials and building functions evaluating the individual object from different perspectives.

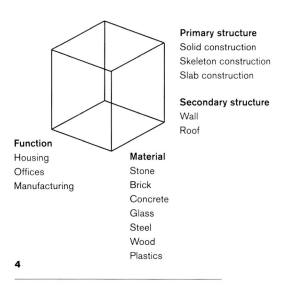

Primary structure
Solid construction
Skeleton construction
Slab construction

Secondary structure
Wall
Roof

Function
Housing
Offices
Manufacturing

Material
Stone
Brick
Concrete
Glass
Steel
Wood
Plastics

4

The space of knowledge of construction
The three-dimensional coordinate system symbolises the three underlying levels of construction.

5

Entry building to Hoge Veluwe nature reserve, Schaarsbergen, Netherlands, MVRDV, 1996
The transition between roof and façade is fluent.

Functions and characteristics of constructions

Buildings are traditionally made up of floors, roofs, columns, outer walls, inner walls, doors, windows, balconies, stairs, and other features. Each of these parts is themselves made up of numerous smaller products and materials. In fact, all these parts are 'components' that together make up the whole, in other words, the building. In this book we limit our description to the highest level of scale: the surfaces that enclose the void or space formed by the building – horizontal, vertical or sloped surfaces. All parts of the building can be regarded as such a surface, or a part thereof. In order to be able to properly understand the nature of the construction, we have to know what function the components fulfil.

Separating function

By setting aside a void that is separate from the infinite and natural space of the outside world, we are able to create conditions that are safer, healthier and more pleasant than those offered by natural spaces. Certain natural or man-made influences are excluded from such a void (rain, for example) or in some cases muted (such as traffic noise). Within the space itself we can also cut ourselves off from others, thus combining the benefits of living close to others with the need for one's own territory, or privacy. We can then carry out activities in such an exclusive space that may be harmful, unsafe or unpleasant for others, or for nature. Separation by means of a construction is the intermediate stage between natural space and a location that has been made habitable. By construction we mean a combination of material parts or components that exist in the same form outside the construction as they do within it, and whose specific material characteristics and shape are largely retained in the construction, and which fulfil a specific functional part of the construction. Examples of non-constructions are for instance:

- a homogenous sheet or plate (there is no composition)
- a sheet with a coat of paint (the coat of paint cannot exist in its own right)
- duplex glue (has two parts but cannot exist in its own right)

So 'construction' here refers to all assembled components and is not restricted to the notion of a support structure. A support structure is that part of the overall construction that is responsible for keeping it in place. The parts of the building form a hierarchical system, in relation to the support function. The primary parts in the fore of this hierarchy can be described as structurally loadbearing: they do not depend on the secondary or tertiary parts. All parts of a building do have a structural support function, as they are subject to gravity, but not all of them perform a crucial part in maintaining the building's structural integrity.

The main function of a construction is to act as an intermediary, as a separating membrane between one space and another. Any outside influence – be it in the form of energy, such as light, heat or sound, or in the form of matter and energy, like raindrops falling at a particular speed, or wind – that comes into contact with a construction can be reflected or absorbed by, or pass through the construction. The sum of the energy or matter that is reflected, accepted or allowed to pass through is always the same as the amount of energy and matter that 'strikes' the construction. In the case of reflection or being allowed to pass through, the influence may remain unaltered, or its direction may change, or it may be dispersed (1).

Reflection   Absorption   Transmission

1

Reflection, absorption and transmission
It is not just light that falls onto glass, but all exterior influences are reflected, absorbed or allowed to pass through.

Any given influence or phenomenon affects not only the conditions on the other side of the construction, but also those on the 'source' side, as well as on the construction itself (2). When designing a construction, we determine the ratio of the phenomenon that is reflected, absorbed and allowed to pass through. We do this for the purpose of influencing the conditions of the space on at least one side of the construction. So when we wish to design a construction, we need to know the following:

- What is the extent and the nature of the phenomenon that we would like to reflect, accept or allow to pass through?
- What are the desired conditions on the 'receiving' side – the conditioned side of the construction? This calls for knowledge of, for example, the circumstances in which people feel comfortable or in which certain processes can best take place. The conditions with which spaces – inside and outside – must comply are in some cases described and quantified in laws and official standards, while commissioning clients or third parties often have extra requirements of their own.
- With what kind of construction can the desired difference in conditions be achieved? This requires knowledge of how materials – and the respective construction composed of these materials – can control influences on both sides to separate internal and external conditions.
- What are the possible effects (negative or otherwise) of certain phenomena on the construction?
- What are the consequences for the non-conditioned side? Designers often focus their attention on the conditions inside the conceived space, disregarding the conditions outside. Attention to these details can be enforced through legislation, but this is lacking in many instances such as exacerbated wind-speeds in the vicinity of high-rises or reflections caused by mirrored glazing.

Loadbearing function

Constructions rely on their permanent structural integrity. Gravity has a universal effect on constructions, but there are also horizontal influences, such as wind loads as well as unexpected occurrences like collisions, fire or explosions. In this context, the necessary function of any construction is its loadbearing function: every construction has to be at least self-supporting, and in many cases support other parts of the building as well. The total of the loadbearing properties ensures that all the forces to which the construction is subject are kept in balance. There is not a single building component that escapes the effects of some force or another, even if it is just gravity. The support functions are distinguished as follows (3).

Strength

All parts of a construction must be sufficiently strong: they cannot give way to any loads that they may be subjected to.

Stability

All parts of a construction must be stable or fixed: the construction as a whole must not fall over, and the individual parts must not tilt or overturn.

Rigidity

All parts of a construction must be sufficiently rigid: they may not become more distorted than is acceptable in terms of how the construction is used.

2

Influences on spatial conditions and on the construction
Exterior and interior influences affect the construction on both sides.

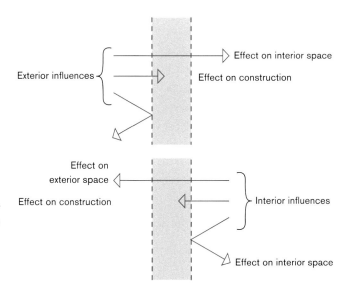

Effect on interior space
Effect on construction
Exterior influences

Effect on exterior space
Effect on construction
Interior influences
Effect on interior space

Properties and performance rate

A function is the intended effect of a construction, or part of a construction. Functions can be divided into objective and subjective functions. The function of a roof, for instance, is to intercept rain, the function of a door is to grant access to the building. Objective functions relate to quantifiable units, subjective functions relate to non-quantifiable ones. For example, 'warm' can be used as an objective term: 38° C is warm, but what constitutes a 'warm' interior is less easy to establish. The performance rate of a component is determined by objective functions only. Once these functions have been established, specific requirements must be assigned to the various components.

These requirements may relate to the properties of the construction. The properties are the clearly definable characteristics of a construction in terms of extent (size and shape) and material composition (4).

The performance rate, or quality, of a construction is the degree to which the characteristics of the construction fulfil the requirements that have been set. The designer determines the characteristics of the construction, and these should meet the relevant requirements (5).

Constructions are usually capable of more than is asked of them – they have over-capacity. However, over-capacity costs money. Constructions may have additional characteristics, which do not support its required performance – or may even have a detrimental effect on it. Building as efficiently as possible means reducing unintended over-capacity and restricting conflicting requirements to a minimum.

The boundaries between different functions of a construction are often blurred. Despite the fact that components such as exterior walls and interior partitions are often categorised as loadbearing or separating parts of a building, their functions and properties are – nonetheless – not confined to merely being loadbearing or separating. A floor slab, for example, has both loadbearing and separating characteristics.

Constructions often only comply with the function they are intended for to a certain degree. The reasons for this may range from poor design to physical feasibility or economic considerations.

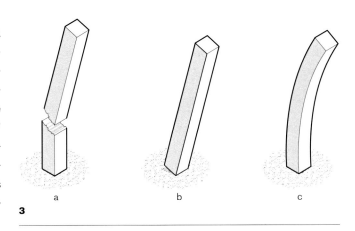

3

The support function of constructions is the sum of strength, stability and rigidity
In case of insufficient strength fracture occurs (a); insufficient stability leads to tilting (b) and insufficient rigidity causes distortion (c).

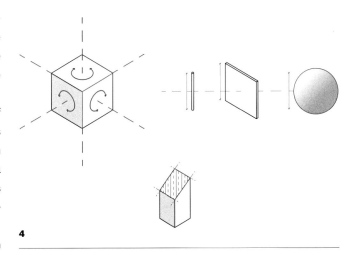

4

Each element of the construction is determined by three characteristics
Position, extent (size and shape) and material

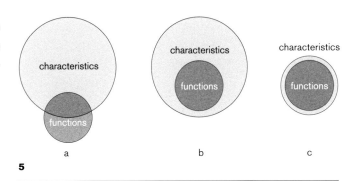

5

The relationship between properties and functions
a The properties do not comply with the requirements. b The properties far exceed the requirements. c Optimisation of requirements and properties.

As long as there is a difference in temperature between two spaces, heat transfer will always occur, and a loadbearing structure will always become distorted in performing its function, even if only very slightly. It is not usually necessary for a building to be absolutely watertight (a building that is extremely watertight will quickly become submerged during floods anyway). Absolute watertightness is also exceedingly costly.

Adjustable and active systems

In some cases the user of a building can influence the ratio between reflection, absorption and transmission in a separating construction. Examples are items that can be opened, like windows (for ventilation and the view), ventilation grids and adjustable sun blinds (6).

In some buildings, certain parameters such as lighting, acoustic performance or ventilation can be controlled by means of active systems.

6

Housing Chassé Park, Breda, Netherlands, OMA, 2000
The constantly changing position of the sunscreens brings buildings to life.

A proportion of solar energy that falls onto buildings is accepted by the construction and then slowly emitted to the surrounding area or the space on the inside. There is currently a lot of work being undertaken to find ways of using some of the energy that envelops buildings for the benefit of the insides of buildings, perhaps with the help of some kind of temporary storage. Examples include photovoltaic (PV) cells that convert light that reaches a building into electrical energy (7), and solar collectors in which warmth from the sun heats up water that can then be used for heating spaces and in hot taps (8).

In the case of buildings with outer wall double glazing, the heated air between the two layers is used for heating spaces.

7

Mont-Cenis Academy, Herne-Sodingen, Germany, Jourda & Perraudin, 1999
Photovoltaic cells convert light into electrical energy and reduce thermal gains.

8

House, Almere, Netherlands, B.J. van den Brink, 1986
Solar collectors convert solar energy into hot water.

Tightness and permeability of constructions

We can make a construction of one layer of material, but then the function that that layer is capable of fulfilling will be decisive for the thickness of the whole construction. By combining layers of different materials, the positive characteristics of each can be enjoyed. That leads to a reduction in building costs, on the one hand because less material is needed in total, and on the other because there is more useful floor space if the outer casing is thinner (9). Also, because the mass of the construction is reduced, the loadbearing constructions such as the foundations do not have to be as strong.

In the table below, a number of materials commonly used in construction are compared with each other in terms of thermal conduction (λ), density, compressive strength and bending strength.

During the course of history there has been a movement from homogenous to multi-layered, multi-scaled and multi-sheeted constructions. Because of research into and the production of materials that can perform better in specific locations, it is possible for tougher requirements to be met. In the case of composite constructions each layer can fulfil a specific function or indeed a combination of functions. Generally, composite solutions

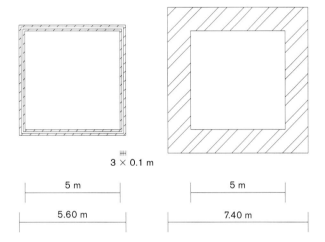

3 × 0.1 m

5 m

5.60 m

5 m

7.40 m

9

Material optimisation in a layered construction
A 5 × 5 m space is surrounded by a cavity wall, 300 mm thick. The gross floor area is 5.60 × 5.60 m = 31 m². The wall is built of brick that is 100 mm thick, with insulation foam 80 mm thick, a 20 mm wide cavity and another layer of brickwork that is 100 mm thick. The thermal insulation value of the air cavity and insulation material is roughly ten times greater than that of stone. If the same insulation value is to be attained using just a brick wall, the 100 mm of insulation and cavity will have to be replaced by 1,000 mm of brickwork. The construction will then be 1,200 mm thick. The gross floor area would be 7.40 × 7.40 m = 54 m² (almost twice as much). The weight of the wall would be 160,000 kg instead of around 25,000 kg (assuming a wall height of 3,000 mm).

	λ [W/MK]	Density [kg/m³]	Compressive strength [N/mm²]	Bending strength [N/mm²]
Steel	52	7,800	200	200
Aluminium	204	2,800	65	65
Granite	2.91	3,000	200	0
Reinforced, compact concrete	2.33	2,500	20	20
Cellular concrete	0.7	1,000	2	0
Pinewood	0.17	550	6.5	7
Mineral wool	0.04	35	0.2	0
Plastic foam	0.035	20	0.3	0

will be chosen in the event that multiple functions with high requirements have to be fulfilled. Constructions can act as a separating membrane through the three main characteristics mentioned previously: the position of the material layers in relation to each other, the dimensions of the layers, and the properties of the materials. The position of the materials in relation to each other is very important for their being able to perform their functions properly and permanently. At this stage, we would like to introduce the term 'functional layer'. A functional layer in a partition construction is a layer that mainly performs a particular function in that construction. Functional layers and material layers are not the same. A material layer can fulfil more than one function, and conversely a function can be performed by more than one material.

The distinction between the two is important because it is not so much the type of material that determines the sequence in which it occurs in a construction, but the function that the material fulfils in the construction.

The material of the functional layer may change within the surface of the exterior wall, for example, where the brickwork meets the window frame, and where the window frame meets the glass. Here, it is always the outermost layer that has the function to resist rain. While material layers only extend to a particular section of the partitional construction, functional layers run continuously over the buildings, including over floors, walls and roofs. Interruptions in these layers are 'leaks': water leaks, air leaks, heat leaks. Changes to the sequence of layers between different building components (such as wall and roof) should always be designed with care as well, as this means that in principle one of the layers will be interrupted (10).

The following section will deal with the functional layers, and the sequence in which such layers should preferably be positioned in a construction. Several examples will then be shown in which the influence of the characteristics of various types of material on the whole construction are highlighted. It is the task of the designer to determine the optimal combination, sequence and thickness of materials, using building physics, materials science and applied mechanics as tools. Without knowledge of these subjects, designers have no choice but to apply tried and tested traditional constructions, without the possibility of translating technological improvements or certain aesthetic wishes that cannot be realised through traditional constructions into a constructive design.

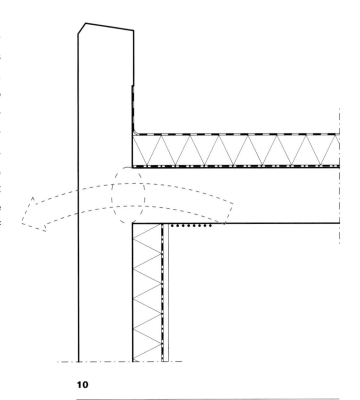

10

Interruption of functional layers
The support structure is in different positions (roof, on the inside; outer wall, on the outside) and interrupts both the thermal insulation and the vapour barrier.

Opaque constructions

Loadbearing layer

In every wall, floor and roof there is always a loadbearing part – a material or composition of materials that fulfils the structural support function and transports horizontal and vertical loads resulting from wind, people, other material layers, as well as its own weight, to the foundations. The layer may be a continuous surface or a framework of linear elements with an infill of subordinate significance.

Thermal insulation

Functionality: Heat transport can take place in three ways – convection, conduction and radiation. Convection occurs only in liquids and gases. Conduction can take place in all materials, while no medium is required for heat exchange in the case of radiation – this can occur in a vacuum. In the building industry, heat insulation is mostly a matter of limiting the conduction of heat, although in some cases it involves restricting radiation.

Heat conductivity is not the same for every material: it can be limited by applying materials with a low heat coefficient. One of the best and least expensive insulators is air. However, the air has to be still, otherwise heat will be exchanged through convection. The thermal insulating capacity of many of the materials used in the building industry is based on motionless air that is trapped inside the pores of the material. Materials with high levels of porosity and therefore a high thermal insulation value are generally mechanically weak. Exceptions include cellular concrete and wood, which are reasonably good insulators and reasonably strong. The more pores, the better the thermal insulation, but the lesser the mechanical strength.

Heat loss can also be reduced by limiting radiation. Heat exchange through radiation depends on the material but more especially the colour and how shiny it is. Aluminium with a smooth polished finish has an emission coefficient of 0.1, compared with 0.98 for a surface that has been painted black (on a scale of 0 to 1). This principle is applied extensively in double glazing. A very thin metal coat is applied to the inner side of the window panes. The layers are so thin that enough light can still pass through. This technique can only be applied if it is possible to guarantee that the layer remains clean – as is the case in the cavity in double glazing.

Positioning: From the above it would appear to be difficult for a single material to perform both the loadbearing and thermal insulation functions. Though it is theoretically possible for a material generally associated with a loadbearing function to be used as a thermal insulator at the same time, this will lead to a noticeably thicker construction than would be the case when functions are split up. Examples include cellular concrete (concrete that contains pores) and wood, which has a naturally high proportion of porosity anyway. On the other hand, there are examples of houses that use styrofoam or strawbales as loadbearing materials.

Wherever the thermal insulation is applied to the inside of the loadbearing structure, the latter will be exposed to relatively wide variations in temperature. Due to their different thermal expansion, tensions will arise at the junctions of parts of the loadbearing structure (exterior walls and roofs) that are exposed to big changes in temperature and those components that are not (floors and internal loadbearing walls) (11).

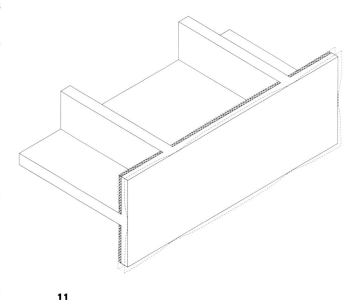

11

Thermal tension at the junctions between loadbearing units
The temperature of the outer wall may be considerably higher as a result of absorption than the outside air temperature. In the case of dark outer walls and roofs this may be as much as 60° C. The interior floor slabs are considerably cooler, which leads to thermal tensions at the junctions.

In addition, thermal bridges occur at these connecting points that result in energy being lost and increase the risk of surface condensation.

In the vast majority of cases, the loadbearing layer is applied inside the thermal insulation. If the material has an open pore structure, it should not be exposed to water, as this would enter the pores and so significantly reduce the thermal insulation value. Thermal insulation materials like mineral wool and glass wool have an open pore structure and absorb water easily. Most plastic foam insulation materials degrade under the influence of UV radiation. In addition, the appearance of thermal insulation materials is not generally acceptable as the outermost visible layer of a construction. These characteristics mean that the thermal insulation layer is almost always applied on the inside of the rain-repellent layer. One exception is the inverted roof (19).

In the case of the inverted roof the thermal insulation layer is attached on top of the waterproofing. The advantage of this arrangement is that it prevents condensation at the underside of the waterproofing course as the temperature there is roughly equal to the interior room temperature; furthermore, the water-proofing is protected from mechanical damage.

Rain screening and waterproofing

Functionality: Two types of materials are used: completely waterproof material and materials that are porous to one degree or another. In the case of the latter, the waterproofing is based on the premise that there will be periods of exposure to water (rainfall) interspersed with dry periods, during which time the rainwater can evaporate. Materials with pores that are larger than water molecules and which are interlinked, absorb water. The water is absorbed deeper and deeper and higher and higher into the material through adhesion and the capillary effect, until a balanced situation is arrived at. Stony materials such as fired brick, natural stone, roof tiles, sand-lime brick and concrete, and wood cut along the direction of the grain which are used for rain screening, are porous and absorb water to a greater or lesser degree, and are therefore not completely waterproof. Applying an extra layer of sealant (glazing or paint) can reduce the level of water absorption. If the material is sufficiently thick, and the construction is not permanently exposed to water pressure, the water can evaporate from the material before it penetrates it completely. These materials are not suitable for horizontal or near-horizontal surfaces.

Metal, glass, bituminous products, rubber and plastic with closed pores cannot be penetrated by water, and they can be used on flat roofs. Another important difference is determined by the joints in the waterproof layers. In the case of flat roofs, they must be absolutely watertight, but this requirement is less stringent for vertical constructions.

Aesthetic demands in relation to exterior walls are generally much higher than those for roofs and this largely explains why designers tend to choose different materials for essentially the same function.

Positioning: The waterproofing layer is almost always the outermost layer of a construction. It protects the construction behind, or underneath it, from the harmful effects of precipitation. Exceptions are discussed at the end of this section. This outermost layer also often has the function of repelling UV radiation, and in addition it must be capable of withstanding mechanical damage. In many cases, especially with outside walls, aesthetic requirements to a large degree determine the choice of material for this outermost layer. The ability to withstand pollution and cleaning properties are also important criteria.

Vapour barrier and air-tightness

Functionality: Water occurs in the atmosphere in three physical states: gas (vapour), liquid (rain) and solid (snow, hail). Water is present in the atmosphere in the form of vapour. The moisture content of the air can be expressed through the vapour density [kg/m^3] or the vapour pressure [N/m^2]. The quantity of vapour that a given amount of air can contain depends on the temperature: warm air can contain more than cold air. The degree to which air is saturated with vapour is given by the relative humidity. This is the ratio of the actual vapour pressure p_w and the saturated vapour pressure p_s at a particular temperature. A relative humidity level of 100% shows that the actual vapour pressure of the air is the same as the saturation pressure and that the air has absorbed the maximum amount of vapour that is possible at that temperature. The temperature at which the relative vapour is 100% is known as the dew point temperature. If the air temperature falls below the dew point temperature, the air will not be able to absorb as much vapour, which will then condense. This will lead to clouds of water droplets in the atmosphere, or if the temperature is below freezing, ice crystals. If the water droplets or ice crystals continue to cool they will become heavier, and gravity will then ensure that they fall downwards as precipitation: snow, hail or rain.

This phenomenon can also occur on or in constructions when the material that comes into contact with the air is colder than the dew point temperature. Vapour condenses on the cold material. We refer to this as surface condensation and internal condensation respectively, and both can lead to damage to materials (decay, corrosion, frost damage), pollution, reduced function (thermal insulation getting wet) and health problems (mould).

Internal condensation: If a construction is colder than the dew point temperature of the surrounding air, condensation will occur on the surface or the interior of the construction. Vapour moves from areas with a high level of vapour pressure to locations where it is lower. The air in warm spaces can absorb more moisture than that in cold spaces. Vapour transport from warm spaces to cold spaces will occur if the partition between the two areas is not airtight, for example as a result of the presence of porous materials or if there is a leak in the construction. Vapour that is transferred through a layer of thermal insulation will cool down on its way from the inside (warm) to the outside (cold). If the air reaches the dew point temperature the vapour there will condense. Water will then be present in the construction. This internal condensation can be prevented by applying a vapour-proof layer on the warm side of the construction. Internal condensation is not a problem if the moisture can evaporate from the construction or be transported outside, before it causes any damage.

In general, the vapour diffusion resistance of the layers on the warm side of the thermal insulation layer should be higher than that of the layers on the cold side of a construction, in order for internal condensation to be prevented. Condensation that has formed in the winter has to be able to evaporate in the warmer months. If the layers on the cold side are completely vapour-proof, there should also be a completely vapour-proof layer on the warm side, while not only the material itself should be vapour-proof, but also the point where the materials meet. This is not always easy to implement in practice and it is also difficult to pinpoint errors that have been made. The waterproof layers on flat roofs are always vapour-proof and that means that in order to prevent internal condensation on the warm side, a vapour barrier layer needs to be applied. This does not have to be a separate material layer. The loadbearing structure (for example a steel plate or concrete) or the layer of thermal insulation (with closed

pores) can also act as a vapour barrier, provided the joints and the connections at the edges of the materials can be made sufficiently vapour-proof. The application of porous 'waterproof' layers would appear to be odd at first, but if we look at the problems relating to internal condensation it seems in many cases to be beneficial.

Cavity: A cavity is a space between two leaves of a construction. The cavity separates the two leaves as far as a number of functions are concerned, although there will always be a mechanical link between the two. In closed (i.e. where light cannot penetrate) parts of the outer wall and the roof, the cavity has primarily a moisture-regulating function. A cavity improves the sound-resistant characteristics of a construction, especially if the two leaves are entirely disconnected. If the amount of water exceeds the absorption capacity of the outer leaf, the inside of the outer leaf will also get wet in the long term. The function of the cavity is then to prevent moisture from reaching the layers on the inner leaf. In cases where the outer leaf is made of a vapour-proof material (metal sheeting, for example) it is possible that in certain circumstances condensation will occur on the inside of the metal. An upwardly directed flow of air in the cavity will remove the moisture. As it is warmer in the cavity than outside, the air in the cavity will rise, and the airflow will lead to an exchange of heat between the inside and outside leaves. The thermal insulation characteristics of ventilated cavities are therefore not great. In the event of water penetrating a sloped or horizontal construction, it will not flow downwards along the outer leaf, but will instead land on the layer of insulation. This has to be protected with a waterproof layer. With sloping roofs this layer can be open to vapour diffusion, but where the roof is flat it must be vapour-proof. The difference between waterproof layers open to vapour diffusion and fully waterproof layers is based on the difference between vapour and liquid water. The surface tension of the liquid prevents water from penetrating the microscopic openings of the vapour-permeable layer, especially if the water is flowing quickly enough. The individual water molecules of the vapour can penetrate the pores. Fully waterproof layers allow neither water nor vapour to pass.

Composite constructions

Composite layers in horizontal, vertical and sloped planes can be arranged in different ways – each with their own specific benefits or limitations. The various types may appear in combined form in one building.

Single-layer arrangement

In this case, one single layer (12) has to be able to fulfil every function. The waterproofness depends very much on the joints in the material. In the case of material without joints (e.g. concrete poured on site) the risk of cracks and resulting disruption to waterproofness is great, especially in sloping and horizontal surfaces.

Separation of loadbearing and thermally insulating layer

This type of arrangement can be subdivided into six categories briefly outlined in the following section.

1. Arrangement without air cavity and with a continous waterproof layer (13):

The continuous waterproof layer on the outside may involve bitumen, PVC or synthetic rubber on the roof and plasterwork on the wall. The need for a vapour barrier in the wall depends on the degree of vapour permeability of the outermost layer. On the horizontal and sloping surface the outermost layer is fully water- and vapour-proof; an effective vapour barrier is required on the warm side of the construction, either as a separate material, or as provided by the loadbearing layer or thermal insulation layer.

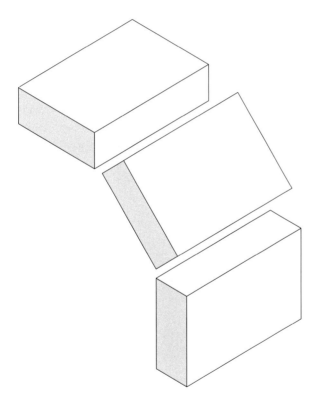

12

Single-layer arrangement
This arrangement is the most simple form of construction.
However, functionality here is most limited.

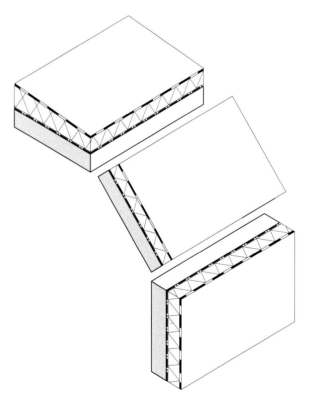

13

Separation of loadbearing and thermally insulating layer without air cavity and with a continous waterproof layer
This build-up is used in constructons such as flat roofs or exterior plastered walls.

2. Arrangement without air cavity and with a waterproof layer with sealed joints (14):

The level of vapour permeability should decrease from the inside towards the outside, and because the outermost layer in the horizontal and sloping part of the surface has to be completely waterproof, the interior has to be moisture-proof. The outermost layer of the wall can be open to moisture which means the requirements in relation to moisture-proofness on the warm side are less stringent. The joints represent a significant leakage risk, especially in horizontal and sloping surfaces. The joints in walls can be given a water-repellent finish on the outside. Because of the risk of leaking, this type is used almost exclusively for vertical walls.

3. Arrangement with ventilated cavity and waterproof layer with sealed joints (15):

Usually, no waterproof layer is required on the outside of the layer of thermal insulation, though this depends on the quality of the joints. If any water does manage to reach the cavity, it will be transported outside at the bottom of the cavity without coming into contact with the thermal insulation. Any leakage water on horizontal or sloping surfaces will fall onto the thermal insulation, rendering it ineffective. Therefore, a vapour-permeable, but waterproof sheeting is required on the thermal insulation. Cold radiation can make thin roof covering (such as metals) very cold, with a risk of surface condensation on the inside of the covering. The condensation may freeze and cause a lot of damage when it thaws. For that reason, too, a good water-repellent layer on the thermal insulation is required to channel water away.

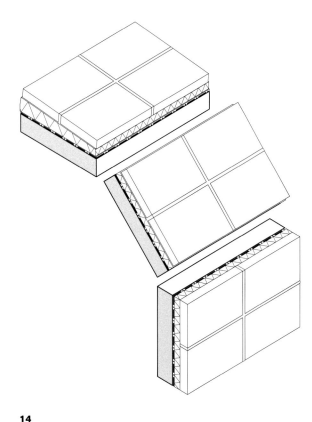

14

Separation of loadbearing and thermally insulating layer without air cavity and with sealed joints
Due to the risk of leakage, this construction is practically not applied for roofs. An exterior wall build-up of this type are tiles glued to Styrofoam.

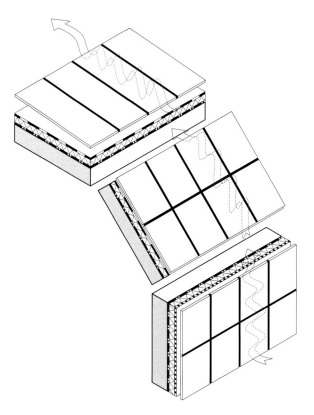

15

Separation of loadbearing and thermally insulating layer with ventilated cavity and sealed joints
This build-up is often used for wall constructions involving metal claddings such as zinc and copper or bricks, but also for sloped tiled roofs. The high risk for leakage renders this type unsuitable for flat roofs.

4. Arrangement with ventilated cavity and open or overlapping joints (16):

This layer also has a mechanical protection function, it offers protection from UV radiation, and serves an aesthetic purpose. On the roof, it can function as a surface on which it is possible to walk, but can also be omitted if the water-repellent layer on the thermal insulation meets the requirements with regard to strength and UV resistance. The water-repellent layer on the thermal insulation in the wall can be of a lesser quality than the one on the roof, as it is not directly affected by water. Sheeting which is open to vapour diffusion, but waterproof, is sufficient here. On the roof, however, good waterproofing and an efficient vapour barrier are necessary.

5. Loadbearing layer with integrated thermal insulation, ventilated cavity and open or overlapping joints (17):

Waterproofing is required behind or under the covering. Sheeting which is open to vapour diffusion, but waterproof, can be used in walls for this purpose – but in roofs, the layer must be fully water- and vapour-proof; in this case a vapour barrier is also required on the internal side. Nowadays, this type of construction is rarely used in roofs (the so-called cold roof) since the risk of internal condensation is too high. Removing moisture that has built up in the construction through ventilation is difficult, unlike in sloping or vertical surfaces.

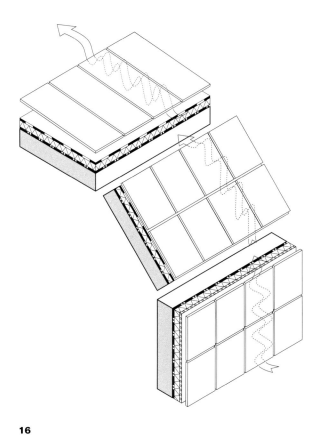

16

Separation of loadbearing and thermally insulating layer with ventilated cavity and open or overlapping joints
The outer layer provides mechanical and UV protection. The waterproofing layer is positioned underneath.

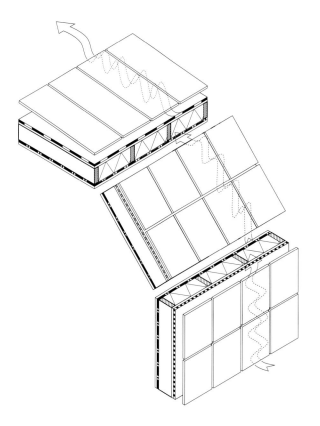

17

Loadbearing layer with integrated thermal insulation with ventilated cavity and open or overlapping joints
This build-up is used in loadbearing and non-loadbearing façade constructions with timber posts.

6. Sandwiched thermal insulation (18):

The outermost layer is waterproof, resists UV radiation and can withstand some mechanical impact. The innermost layer should therefore be vapour-proof as well, as should the thermal insulation, or there should at least be a vapour-proof layer between the inner layer and the thermal insulation. The connections between the panels on horizontal and sloping surfaces are particularly complex and susceptible to leaks. The finish on the joints in vertical surfaces should enable water to drain off. This construction uses sandwich panels in a post-and-beam system.

Inverted roof

The thermal insulation is plastic foam with closed pores (19). It cannot be penetrated by water, although water can get in through the joints between the insulation panels and along the edges. To avoid this, the panels can be glued together. Water that does get in forms a thin, thermally conductive layer under the insulation, but in theory that is no problem as the thermal insulation continues to be present. The water that is absorbed by the panels has to be able to evaporate. The plastic foam remains in position thanks to gravel ballast, which also protects against UV radiation. A good gradient (>1%) is a precondition for this construction to function properly, while another benefit is that the roof can be waterproofed very quickly.

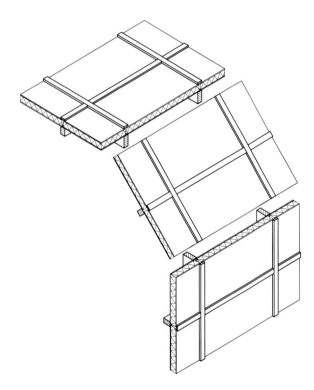

18

Sandwiched thermal insulation
Sandwich panels are mostly used for wall constructions. Due to the risk of leakage and difficult drainage they are rarely applied to sloped roofs and practically never to flat roofs.

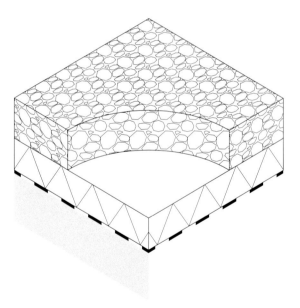

19

Inverted roof
The insulating layer is positioned on top of the waterproofing course to provide mechanical protection. This means that the insulating layer has to resist UV radiation or else must be protected from it.

Transparent constructions

Glass is by far the most frequently used material for transparent constructions (20).

Loadbearing structure

Since the early 1980s, experiments have been carried out with glass as a loadbearing structure (21), but in the vast majority of cases it will not act as primary structure – it will only be part of a complementary system. Glass is very strong, comparable with steel, but that level of strength is sharply reduced if any damage to the surface occurs, which makes it unsafe and puts it in the category of a fragile material. By thermal or chemical toughening of glass, the strength can be increased. Safety levels can be improved by applying transparent laminated glazing films. This does not make the glass that much stronger, but the artificial film prevents the glass from shattering when it breaks.

Light permeability

Light permeability is expressed by the absolute light entry factor. The visible light transmission is the ratio between the amount of light that passes through the glass and that which lands on it. Additionally, the solar transmission factor oder solar gain (g-value) is important: in the case of glazing systems this is the ratio between the sun's rays that pass through the glass, and those that are absorbed by it. The light transmission relates to visible light, and the g-value to all solar rays, including infrared and ultraviolet radiation.

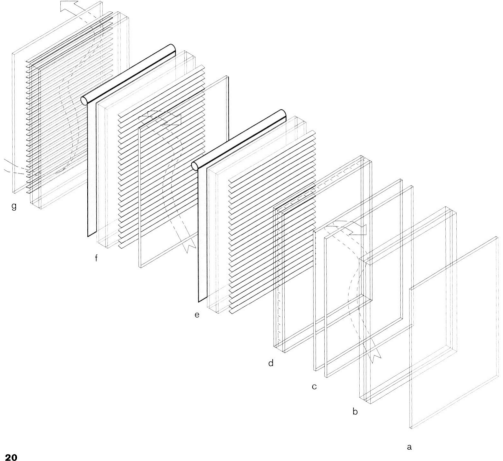

20

Possible build-up of transparent constructions with glass
a Single glazing
b Laminated glazing
c Double glazing with a ventilated cavity
d Insulating double glazing with sealed cavity
e Insulating double glazing with sealed cavity and metal coating on the inside
f Double façade
g Exhaust cavity façade

Thermal insulation

Glass and transparent plastics have a high heat conductivity. Moreover, because of the thin layers of these materials used in transparent single-leaf constructions they provide low thermal insulation. The thermal insulation effect can be increased by applying two layers with a gap of motionless air between them.

If the connection between the two panes of glass is not airtight, the air between the two layers may condense in the cavity. The condensation will disappear when heated but will leave dirt behind. The two panes have to be separable in order for the cavity to be cleaned. Normally, however, the connection between the two glass panes is airtight and the air in the cavity is so dry that no condensation occurs when the temperature cools sharply. The thermal insulation can be improved by applying a thin layer of transparent silver with a low radiation emission on the cavity side of the inner leaf. This lowers the g-value so that the space behind the glass does not heat up as much. This can be a disadvantage, because this also lowers the amount of daylight that can penetrate, but in office buildings with a lot of glass and a high internal heat load, it is an advantage. The air in the cavity can be replaced by an inert gas (argon).

Noise resistance

Glass has a high specific mass, roughly similar to that of concrete (2,500 kg/m³). As it is not very thick it is not particularly noise-resistant. Noise may be reduced by applying either mass as such or a mass-spring system: the latter is based on two material layers of different mass and a noise-insulating interlayer (as in sandwich elements).

Applying thermally insulating glazing, preferably with panes of different thickness, improves the level of noise resistance considerably.

Solar protection

When solar energy passes through a glass construction and reaches an interior space, the energy will heat up the walls, floors, ceilings and all the objects in that space. These in turn will emit energy in the form of long-wave heat, which is then unable to pass back outside through the thermally insulating glazing. As a result the space heats up: the greenhouse effect. In order to prevent this heating-up process, sun-resistant screens must be placed in front of the glass on the outside. However, these screens are susceptible to the effects of wind, and maintaining them is expensive, in particular in high-rises. In addition, sunscreens obscure the view, although this depends on the type that is used.

This has led to the development of two types of façade systems. These are used mostly in buildings with a high internal heat load, such as office buildings.

21

Glass House, Almere, Netherlands, Benthem Crouwel Architecten, 1984
The roof is supported by the façade glazing.

1. Exhaust cavity façade (22): The cavity is enclosed by thermal double glazing on the outside and single glazing on the inside. Sun-resistant blinds are placed in the cavity. The heat that is now created in the cavity is removed via the building's ventilation system and may be recycled (immediately, for example on the north side of the building) or, in the winter, stored for heating. The main purpose of the exhaust cavity façade is to prevent the spaces behind it from overheating. The interior pane can be accessed for cleaning and maintenance. The cavity is 100 to 300 m deep.

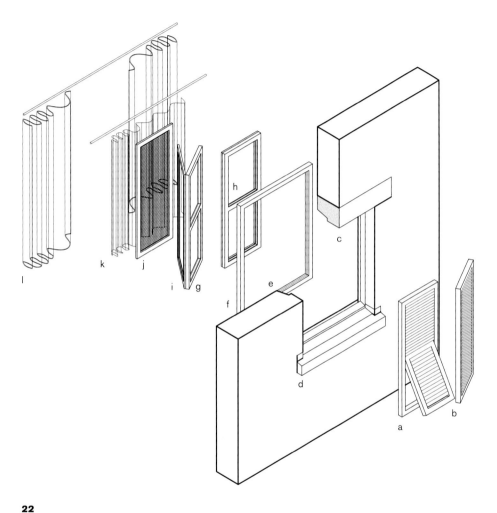

22

Double casement window as a precursor of the exhaust cavity façade
a Window shutters provide burglary prevention and block out light.
b Folding shutters provide views onto the street.
c Lintel transfers loads to both sides of the window.
d Dripstone carries water via an overhang across the outer wall, so that the wall does not get dirty.
e Angled soffits mitigate the contrast between window and wall.
f Window frame as transitional construction from wall to glass or operable window
g Windows that open inwards provide ventilation and allow to operate the shutters from the inside.
h Glazing bars can be used to divide a window pane.
i Double windows provide extra thermal insulation during winter and prevent ice from forming on the inside of the window. It must be possible to open or remove the double window in order for it to be cleaned. Improved noise protection.
j Insect mesh
k Net curtains soften the contrast, provide privacy and decoration, keep insects out.
l Curtains intercept light and provide decoration, greater absorption of noise.

2. Double-skin façade (23): The inside of the cavity consists of a double layer of glass, and the outside of a single layer. Sunscreens are placed in the cavity. Here, too, the purpose is to protect the space behind the window from overheating. However, the cavity in this case is ventilated using outside air. The air that is heated inside the cavity may be used for heating the building.

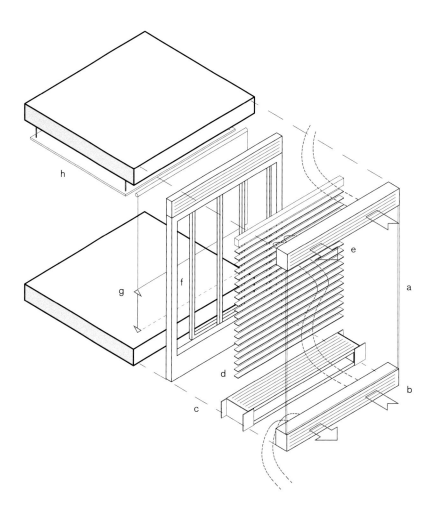

23

Double-skin façade
a Single pane of toughened glass, frameless. Provides wind protection, rain protection, and, in combination with a cavity and inner window pane, noise protection.
b Grill/flaps (with insect mesh) supply air for ventilation of cavity.
c Cavity acts as heat buffer and is accessible for maintenance and possibly permanent use as additional space.
d Louvre slats, rotatable, possibly vertically operable, centrally controlled, provide heat protection.
e Air is ventilated directly outside or heat is reclaimed.
f Frame with doors that can be opened to allow access to and/or ventilation of the cavity
g Individually controlled glare protection for improved desktop working environment
h Suspended ceiling hiding technical services, lighting fittings and providing control of sound levels

Loadbearing behaviour

The primary demand we make of every construction is that they remain in the location and form of their design – in other words, that they are able to resist the effects of forces working against them. In order to be able to understand the structure of walls, roofs and floors, it is necessary to know something about mechanics and the strength of materials.

Force and tension

When we exercise traction on a rope, the level of traction in the rope is the same as that being exercised on it. If we pull on the rope even harder, there will come a point when it snaps. If we use a thicker rope, we will have to pull more strongly (exercise greater traction) in order to tear the rope apart. What determines whether the rope tears or not is therefore not just the strength in the rope, but its thickness. This ratio between applied force and the diameter ('thickness') is referred to as tension. Tension (σ) in [N/m²] is defined as the force (F) in [N] per unit of surface area (A) [m²].

The tension in a material increases the greater the strength and the smaller the surface area. The rope will break if the tension exceeds a given limit, the admissible level of traction. The admissible level of traction is a material characteristic which varies from one material to another.

If a rope is pulled with equal force from both sides, forces are in equilibrium. The forces act along the same axis, but in opposite directions.

1 Yield point
2 Rupture
3 Yield stress
4 Maximum stress
5 Angle that indicates E

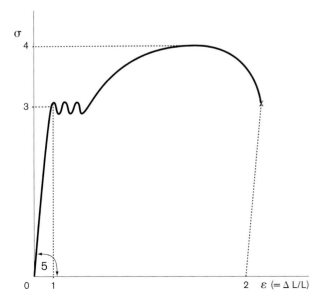

Elasticity

By pulling on the rope, it will become longer. If we stop pulling, it will become shorter again. The rope behaves more or less like an elastic band. We refer to this as elastic deformation. The lengthening is directly proportional (up to a certain limit) to the tension in the material. Conversely, a rod will become shorter if we push on it, and longer when we relax the pressure. The degree of deformation depends on the material of which the rod is made. The modulus of elasticity or Young's modulus [E] is a material constant that serves as a measure for elastic deformation. The greater the value E, the stiffer the material is.

The ratio between tension, distortion and material is shown in Hooke's law:

$$\Delta L/L = \sigma/E$$
L is the length of the object,
ΔL is the change in length.

Material is distorted when we exercise a force upon it, no matter how small. If the tension is very high in relation to the admissible level of tension, plastic deformation can occur in addition to elastic deformation. In the case of plastic deformation, the distortion that has been induced remains present even after the force that created it has been removed. Different materials behave in very different ways as their limits are approached – some show no plastic deformation at all (they break as soon as a certain limit is exceeded), others do. These materials first distort considerably (when the force being exercised is constant) before the point of rupture is reached (24). They are safe because they warn before they do so. Some materials can absorb compressive stress very well, while others can absorb both tensile stress and compressive stress, although there may be a difference between the admissible levels for each. There are no materials that can handle a lot of tensile stress but little compression.

24

Stress-strain diagram for steel
As the stress increases, the distortion initially increases proportionally. Distortion then occurs without the stress increasing. The material then stabilises and finally reaches the point of rupture.

It is said of wood that it is not as capable of absorbing tensile stress as it is of compressive stress, but that is primarily due to the difficulty in making joints that are capable of withstanding tension rather than to the material itself. Materials can be isotropic (that is, that the characteristics are the same in every direction) or anisotropic. In the case of the latter, there may be considerable differences between the admissible levels of tension, the E modulus or Young's modulus and other characteristics in the various directions. Wood is a good example of this. The acceptable compressive stress in the direction of the grain may be as much as eight times greater than perpendicular to it, depending on the type of wood in question (25).

Buckling

An important phenomenon as far as elements that are subject to compression are concerned is that of buckling. If we pull on a rope that is sagging, the sag will be reduced, and the harder we pull, the straighter the rope will become. However, if we push on a thin, relatively long rod, this will suddenly buckle and almost immediately break before the maximum permissible tension that applies to the material has been reached.

The slenderness is a particular ratio between the length of the rod on the one hand, and the shape and the dimensions of the diameter on the other. The longer the rod, the greater the slenderness and the quicker a buckle will occur. Also of significance is how the rod is attached on both sides (26).

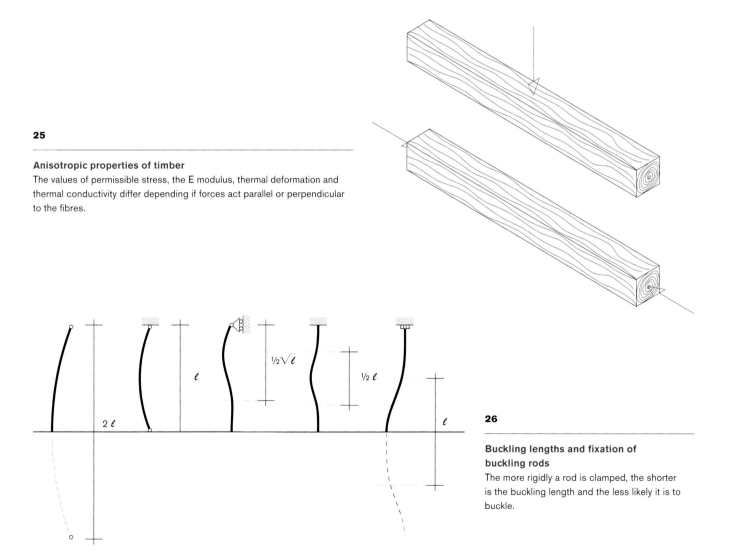

25

Anisotropic properties of timber
The values of permissible stress, the E modulus, thermal deformation and thermal conductivity differ depending if forces act parallel or perpendicular to the fibres.

26

Buckling lengths and fixation of buckling rods
The more rigidly a rod is clamped, the shorter is the buckling length and the less likely it is to buckle.

Span constructions

Vertical loads on span constructions can be transferred via the axial forces of tensile stress and compressive stress and via bending (27).

Span constructions subject to tension

We can bend a rope in any direction without any trouble. In architectural terms we say that a rope is not capable to withstand bending forces, that it offers no resistance to bending. However, a rope can transfer tensile stress. In a rope that is hanging between two points, the rope is only subject to axial forces along its length. There is only tensile stress in the rope. At the points where the rope is attached (at the bearings), the resultant force must be equal but diametrical to the force in the rope. The reaction can be split into a horizontal and a vertical component. The more the rope is tightened, the more the horizontal component of the counterforce increases (28).

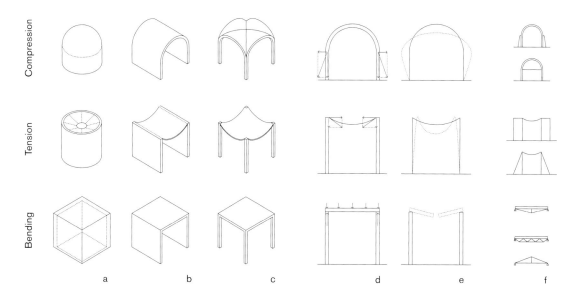

27

Overview of span construction types
Top row: span constructions subject to compression
Middle row: span constructions subject to tension
Bottom row: span constructions subject to bending
a Solid construction
b Slab construction
c Skeleton construction
d Force path
e Deformation
f Structural design solution

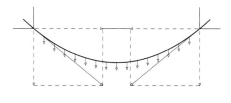

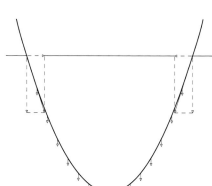

28

Counterforces in a tightened rope
The tighter the rope is pulled, the greater the horizontal forces on the supports.

The best-known type of tensile span constructions are suspension bridges. Huge spans can be created using very little material and basic technology (29).

One problem is the transfer of the horizontal component of the counterforce, and this can only be solved using complex and often heavy bearings in the ground. Another disadvantage is that the vertical clearance is the smallest in the middle of the space. This method of construction is not often applied in buildings, although there are a number of notable examples, such as the Portuguese Pavilion at the World Exhibition in Lisbon (30, 31).

The resulting horizontal forces are accepted by the large weight of the two building masses at both sides of the span.

A derived form are the tensioned constructions for storage warehouses and factories that were commonly applied in the final quarter of the 20th century by 'high-tech' architects Sir Norman Foster, Sir Richard Rogers and Nicholas Grimshaw. Only materials that can absorb tension are applicable for this type such as plant fibres wound into ropes, steel and aluminium.

29

Suspension bridge in Norway
Large spans can be achieved with little effort, but securing it places heavy demands on the foundations.

30

Portuguese Pavilion, World Exhibition, Lisbon, Alvaro Siza, 1998
There are tensile stresses in the roof, while the buildings on both sides provide the counterforces.

31

Portuguese Pavilion, World Exhibition, Lisbon, Alvaro Siza, 1998
The cables that have been sunk into the concrete accept the tensile stress.

Span constructions subject to compression

Before builders had steel at their disposal, many span constructions were made of stone. There are still many impressive stone constructions in the world (33) – in temples (32), churches and civil structures like bridges and aqueducts (34). However, stone can only accept compressive forces. Building stone constructions in the form of an arch creates only compressive forces. The effect is exactly reversed to tensile span constructions: if these are built with cables or chains, they adopt their shape automatically and will only be subject to tensile stress. In order to ascertain the most ideal shape for his design of the Sagrada Familia in

32

Pantheon, Rome, Hadrianus, 118–125 AD
Dome with a span of 43 m transferring loads into circular walls

33

Stone arch constructions in an old barn in France, 1820
The wooden beams have given way; the thin arch, which is no longer stabilised, is still intact.

34

Pont du Gard, Nîmes, 52 AD
Stone arch construction using a row of continuous, stacked arches to span the valley. Arches transfer vertical loads below and resulting horizontal forces are transferred into the sides of the valley.

Barcelona, Antonio Gaudí used so-called chain models (35). The models were an inversed model of the eventual construction subject to compression.

The arches are composed of natural stone or bricks which may or may not be cemented together or – in the case of a natural stone – joined with bronze pins. If the joint between the stones is perpendicular to the line on which the normal force in the arch exerts its effect, there is a balance of forces in the joint and the composition is stable. As in the case of constructions based on tensile stress, there are horizontal forces in the supports, but here they are directed outwards. The flatter the arch, the greater the resulting horizontal force. These outwardly directed horizontal forces must be in balance with each other (36). If they cannot be directly supported by the foundations, other

35

Chain model of the Sagrada Familia, Barcelona, Antonio Gaudí, 1882–1926
It is almost impossible to simulate in a model the most ideal form of the arches, especially in an assembled construction. By inverting the structural tension and turning the model upside down, hanging from a floor using chains, the form of the building can be seen in which only normal forces occur. By applying wax or lacquer to the chains, the model can be inverted, creating a construction in which only compression occurs.

measures must be taken, such as the provision of tensile rods or supporting pillars. The advantage is in the small quantity of material that is needed to make the span, in comparison to a construction based on bending forces. An obvious drawback is the great height of the construction and the fact that the top of the construction is not flat.

Until the use of iron (late 18th century) and later steel (since the mid-19th century) and reinforced concrete (in the late 19th century), the preferred material for large spans was stone. It is difficult to obtain wood of sufficient length and durability, and the susceptibility of wood to weather influences is much greater than is the case with stone.

Span constructions subject to bending forces

When we lay a plank on two support points and then stand on it, it will bend downwards. The downward force is as great as the sum of the two forces directed upwards (37). If we lift up a weight with one arm and then stretch the arm, we can feel the weight becoming heavier the more we stretch the arm out (38). What we experience is a momentum. A moment [M] in a particular point is the product of the force [F] and the distance [a] to that point.

$$M = F \cdot a$$

There are no external horizontal forces on the plank so it does not change length (in accordance with Hooke's law). If we exert further pressure on the curve, we see that the underside of the beam becomes longer and the top side shorter, but on average the length of the plank will remain the same.

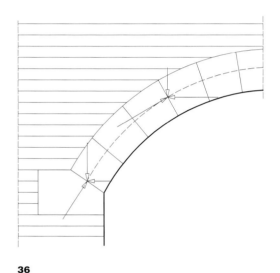

36

Load transfer in an arch construction
The arches are not subject to bending forces. Loads are transferred via compression.

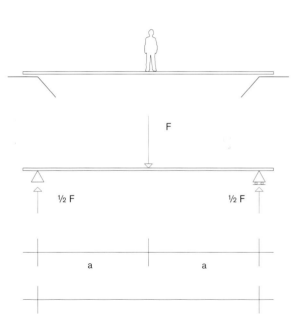

37

External forces in balance in a girder supported on two points
The force downwards is equal to the sum of the counterforces. The force directed downwards lies on the same axis as the resulting upward directed forces.

Clearly there is compression in the upper side of the plank that makes it shorter, and tension in the underside that makes it longer (39). If we conduct a section through the centre of the plank at the point of the greatest load, the resulting moment $\frac{1}{2} F \cdot \frac{1}{2} \ell$ caused by the bearing force becomes visible: theoretically this should cause the plank to rotate.

However, as the plank does not rotate there is obviously another moment involved. This moment within the plank is just as great – but is operating in the opposite direction – as the $\frac{1}{2} F_A \cdot \frac{1}{2} \ell$ moment. The tensile stress in the underside of the plank and the compression in the top side act together, providing the moment that keeps the plank in balance (40). Along the middle axis of the plank, the deformation is zero – therefore the stress equals zero there, too. The top and bottom show the greatest deformation, hence stress is greatest there. The stress along the section diagrammatically has a triangular shape.

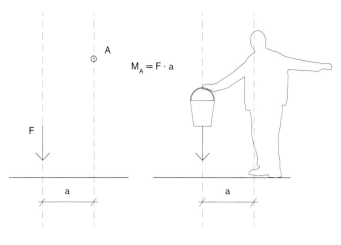

38

Moment, force and lever arm
The example of a water bucket lifted by an outstretched arm illustrates how the force in the (lever) arm creates a moment.

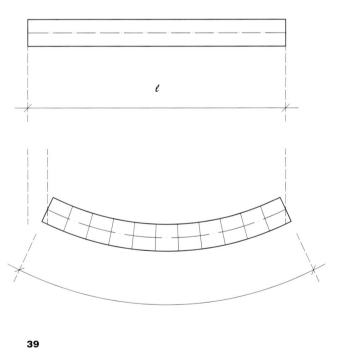

39

Deflection in a girder
The girder is shortened on the top side and stretched on the underside. Since the total length remains the same, the tangential length of the curved girder is shorter than the length of the straight girder.

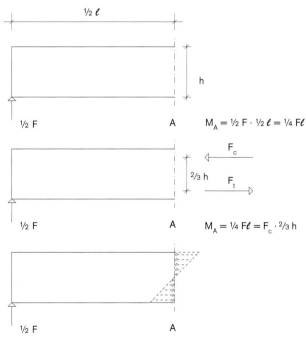

40

External and internal equilibrium of forces within a girder
The external load ($\frac{1}{2} F$) creates a bending moment in point A resulting in internal counter-forces (stress and compression). This keeps the forces in balance.

As the load on the plank increases, stress will increase and the bending moment will be greater, resulting in further deformation (41). When the stress exceeds the permissible level, the plank will break.

We have described here a plank with a load in the middle, but have neglected to consider the weight of the plank. In practice, this dead load of constructions forms an important part in structural design. Often, the changing loads do not occur at particular points, but are evenly distributed along the length of the girder.

In the case of a point load, the bending moment at the centre of the plank is ¼ Fℓ. Without further digression, we can state that with a plank on two support points, the bending moment in the middle is:

$$M = \frac{1}{8} q\ell^2$$

where

q is the evenly distributed load in [N/m¹] and ℓ the span of the plank in [m].

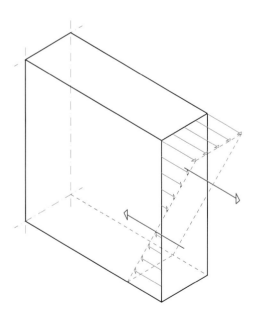

Diagram of stress in a homogenous girder subject to bending forces
The stress in the middle of the profile is zero, but at its maximum at the extreme top and bottom.

From this formula it appears that the moment increases potentially with the squared span (ℓ), provided the load is evenly distributed. A doubling of the span therefore produces a fourfold increase of the bending moment. It also appears that the bending moment does not depend on the shape of the section or the material properties of the plank.

The plank breaks if the tension in it exceeds the permissible level of tension. The tension in the plank is represented by the following formula:

$$\sigma = \frac{M}{Z} \quad (1)$$

in which

σ is the tension, [N/mm²],
M the bending moment [Nm] and
Z a form factor, the elastic section modulus or moment of resistance.

The moment of resistance for a rectangular section is

$$\frac{1}{6} bh^2 \quad (2)$$

in which

b is the breadth of the plank and h is the height.

If we combine (1) and (2), we can see the relationship between stress and shape of the section:

$$\sigma = \frac{M}{\frac{1}{6} bh^2}$$

From this formula we can deduce that – providing the load remains constant – doubling the breadth will halve the tension, but that by doubling the height, the tension in the plank will decrease to ½ · ½ = ¼. It is therefore more economical to position a girder upright rather than putting it on its side.

The formula for the maximum deflection of a plank on two supporting points, bearing an evenly distributed load is:

$$f = \frac{5}{384} \frac{q\ell^4}{EI}$$

in which:

f is the elastic deflection [m]
q is the evenly distributed load [N/m^1]
ℓ is the span [m]
E is the elasticity modulus of the material.
I is a form factor, the moment of inertia; with a right-angled cross-section, this is

$$\frac{1}{12} bh^3$$

From this formula we can deduce that the deflection is in proportion to the power of four of the span – so doubling the span increases the deflection 16 times.

It also appears that the height of the plank is of even greater influence on the deflection than its strength. The deflection is inversely proportional to the breadth of the plank and inversely proportional to the power of three of the height. Note: the height [h] is not the largest cross-sectional dimension but that of the direction in which the load is borne (42).

These laws do not only apply to horizontal girders, but also to columns in outer wall constructions and columns that have to withstand horizontal forces, such as the wind.

It therefore makes economic sense to make beams high and narrow. However, if the height-to-breadth ratio is too great, other effects will come into play (tilting, buckling), which means there is a limit to how much the height-to-breadth ratio can be increased by (43).

The form of many types of floors and walls is determined by these laws.

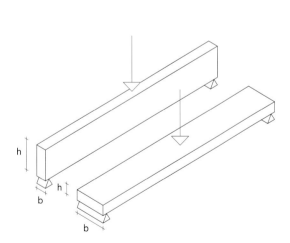

42

Comparison of vertical section and horizontal section
Height h of a beam is the dimension in the direction of the force on the beam.

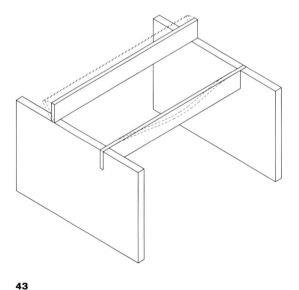

43

Tilting and buckling
Tilting is where the girder is unstable; buckling is where the girder bends on the side where the compressive forces are the greatest.

The diagram of stress – based on a rectangular section supported on two points and with an evenly distributed load – shows that the stress is greatest in the outermost fibres, due to the bending moment. In the rest of the section the material is stressed below capacity. This has led to the standard profiles of some materials (especially steel and aluminium) being shaped accordingly (44).

In the case of concrete hollow core slabs the material has been removed from the centre of the cross-section as well since it would only add unnecessary weight to the slabs and hardly contribute to their strength. In the case of timber and concrete the manufacture of I or H sections is relatively expensive and is therefore applied less often, and only in the case of larger spans, when the high manufacturing cost is justified by the savings in weight. From the above it appears that the position and shape of loadbearing elements are of significant influence on strength and rigidity (45).

The fact that the height of a beam determines to a significant degree its loadbearing capacity and, even more so, its degree of deformation, has an impact on many floor and wall systems. If, for instance, the beams in a floor are used upright (46), the stiffness and strength increase and fewer beams are needed. The gaps between the beams have to be closed in order to create a floor that can be walked on, but as the span between the beams

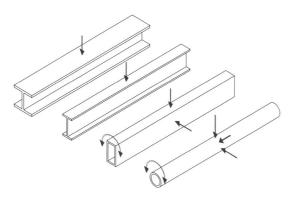

44

H profile, I profile, box and round section
Steel constructions are made as standardised H and I profile, box and round sections. H and I profiles are used where there is a load mainly in one direction, and box and round sections when the profile faces loads from two directions or when there is torsion.

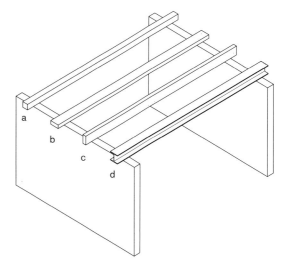

45

Section and position of girders
Depending on the profile shape, girders will alter their loadbearing capacity. When applied correctly material savings can be achieved.
a Solid section
b Horizontal position with reduced loadbearing capacity
c Vertical position with heightened loadbearing capacity
d Standard profile with reduced material use

is small, the amount of material that is needed is much less than what would be gained by rotating the beams. Many types of floors and walls feature this kind of graduated weight dispersion, sometimes in a structure with several levels of main beams and bridging joists (47).

The uppermost layer may be an addition that does not possess a primary loadbearing function, but if it is connected firmly enough to the beams, it fulfils an important secondary role as support of the flooring.

Three factors can limit the usefulness of this method. First, these floors do not have a flat underside, which can cause a problem in terms of creating soundproof connections of interior walls. Also, the reduction in weight can lead to the floor not being sufficiently heavy to absorb structure-borne noise, and finally there are aesthetic arguments for making the undersides of floors or ceilings flat. Fitting a flat, suspended ceiling can be very costly, thus making floor material and weight savings obsolete in the first place.

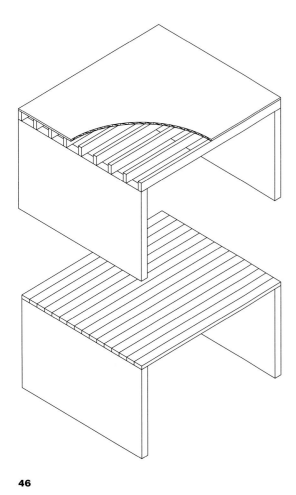

46

Economic use of material in floor constructions
The floor is made up of flat beams which are three times as wide as they are high. If we rotate the beam, it is 3^2 times stronger (the height squared) and 3^3 times more rigid.

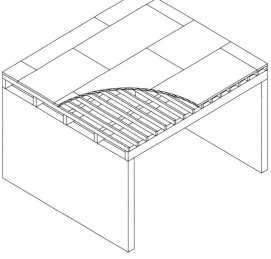

47

System consisting of primary and secondary beams
The deck consists of multiple loadbearing layers of primary and secondary beams.

Horizontal constructions

The typological classification of horizontal constructions is based on the types of available support of the construction: linear, all-round (solid construction method), linear in two directions (slab construction method) and on columns (skeleton construction method). The span can be achieved using any construction subject to compression, tension or bending. At this stage we mainly focus on constructions subject to bending forces.

In each of these types it is possible to choose, in theory, a construction with a flat top and underside, slabs using profiled girders or decks, or a frame system consisting of primary members and secondary elements spanning the spaces between the primary elements.

Two-way slabs, all-round support (solid construction method), flat slab

	Description	Span up to	Application	
	Flat in situ concrete slab, with main reinforcement in two directions.	8 m	Ground floor, upper storey, roof	Much freedom for apertures and overhangs. Insertion of cables possible, depending on the diameter.
	Filigree floor slab. The concrete is poured on prefabricated concrete slabs that also serve as shuttering. Filigree base and in situ concrete form a solid compound. The main reinforcement runs in one direction in the filigree slab, and in the other direction in the in situ concrete slab. The reinforcement in the filigree slab can be prestressed. This can also be done in the top layer, but it has to be done on site, which is much more complicated.	9.50 m	Upper storey, roof	Prefabricated floor. Much freedom for apertures and overhangs. Insertion of pipes possible, depending on the diameter.
	BubbleDeck floors. Like the filigree floor slab, except that plastic balls are inserted into the floors, so that the height of the construction is greater, assuming the same weight. This means bigger spans can be achieved.	15 m	Upper storey, roof	Prefabricated floor. Much freedom for apertures and overhangs. Insertion of pipes possible, depending on the diameter.

Two-way slabs, all-round supports, solid construction method, slabs with a coffered underside

	Description	Span up to	Application	
	Coffered ceiling. Plastic coffers are placed on flat shuttering, and reinforcement is applied between and over the coffers whereupon the concrete is poured. This type of floor is rarely used nowadays.	15 m	Upper storey, roof	Much freedom for apertures and overhangs.

	Description	Span up to	Application	
	Space frames. Consisting of steel rods, with a relatively great structural height. The joints in the rods may be prefabricated off-the-shelf systems or custom-made.	40 m	Roofs	Large overhangs possible, up to 30% of the span.

In addition to these conventional methods, there are special solutions for certain projects, involving the use of timber, concrete or steel. It is important to consider at the design stage that spanning a space in two directions with linear elements produces a confrontation between the linearity of the spanning elements and the span in two directions. The loadbearing elements must cross each other. Making a sufficiently strong and above all rigid structural joint is costly and therefore only possible in exceptional buildings (48).

Occasionally, continuous primary girders are used in timber structures spanning in one direction, and interrupted girders – resting on the former ones – in the other direction. This applies to half-lap joints which – strictly speaking – lead to constructions which no longer span in two ways. In a half-lap joint, a lot of material has to be removed at the junction of the girders. Thus, this weakened point of the profile determines the strength of the overall girder (49).

In steel constructions, the connection can be welded or bolted. On-site welding is awkward, while bolted constructions are generally subject to strong deformation (due to the concentration of the forces) and do not readily lend themselves to achieving particularly elegant connections.

Perpendicular beams can be made of in situ concrete, but a preferred method in simple constructions is to use prefabricated concrete constructions due to the high cost of the shuttering and the longer time needed to allow the concrete to harden.

48

Connection between radial timber beams
The connection is created by a welded steel pin, which is bolted to the wooden beams. The image illustrates the complexity and to-be-expected cost of this joint.

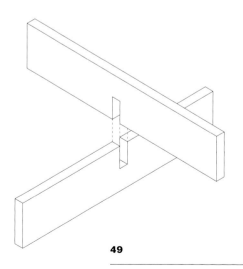

49

Half-lap joint
The cross-section of the beam is halved at the point where the loads are largest.

Flat, one-way slabs, solid construction method, flat slab

	Description	Span up to	Application	
	Even in situ concrete floor slab with reinforcement in one direction.	8 m	Ground floor, upper storey, roof	Much freedom for apertures and overhangs. Insertion of cables possible, depending on the diameter.
	Filigree floor slab. The concrete is poured on site on prefabricated concrete slabs that also serve as shuttering. Slab and in situ concrete form one entity. The main reinforcement is in one direction in the slab. The reinforcement in the slab can be prestressed.	9.50 m, prefab parts' width 2,500 mm	Upper storey, roof	Prefabricated floor. Much freedom for apertures and overhangs due to possibility of applying extra reinforcement to the floor. Insertion of cables possible, depending on the diameter.
	Solid, prefabricated concrete floor slab.	10 m, element width 1,200 mm	Upper storey, roof	No overhangs possible. Limited recess in floor. Apertures possible by using trimmer beams.
	Concrete hollow core slabs.	18 m, element width 1,200 mm, made-to-measure covers	Ground floor, upper storey, roof	Prefabricated floor. Limited apertures in the floor, no overhangs. Apertures possible by using trimmer beams.
	Wing floor slab. Prefabricated concrete floor consisting of a lightweight concrete slab part, 1,200 mm wide, and two thin wings on both sides, each 600 mm wide. Cables can be laid on the lower parts before the slab is cast.	15 m	Upper storey	Prefabricated floor. Limited apertures in the floor.
	Solid glue-lam floor slab of laminated wood. Usually five layers are glued onto and next to each other. The layers lie perpendicular to each other, with the outermost ones in the direction of the span.	6 m	Upper storey, roof	Small apertures are possible, depending on the load. Trimming joints with the help of auxiliary structures.

One-way slabs, skeleton construction method, profiled slabs or decks

	Description	Span up to	Application	
	Ribbed slab. Prefabricated floor slabs, 1,200 mm wide, consisting of a concrete slab with two parallel ribs along the sides.	7.50 m	Mostly as ground floor for residential buildings. The slab is usually given a layer of thermal insulation when manufactured.	Apertures can only be made in the space between the ribs. No overhangs possible.
	Double-T slabs. Prefabricated concrete slab with two parallel ribs on the underside. The difference to the ribbed slab is that the ribs are not on the edges of the slabs. This allows greater freedom in terms of the form of the edges of the slab.	28 m, depending on the load	Upper storey, roofs of larger spans	Apertures only in the space between the ribs.
	Steel deck composite slab. Steel (or concrete) girders with corrugated metal deck on top, onto which the concrete is cast. The metal deck acts as lost shuttering and reinforcement for tensile stress at the same time.	5.50 m without intermediate support points	Upper storey, roof	Temporary supports required during pouring stage. Apertures depend on load and span dimensions. Reinforcement can be laid at the location of the apertures, or extra joists can be used.

One-way slabs, solid construction method, linear girders and infill

	Description	Span up to	Application	
	Polystyrene insulation floor. Prefabricated concrete beams (distance between the centre points of each, 600 mm), with EPS filling between them, covered by concrete topping with shrinkage reinforcement.	5.50 m	Ground floor	Apertures between the beams or by making special trimmer constructions.
	Composite girder slab. Reinforced load-bearing floor consisting of a concrete bottom shell (70 mm thick) and cast-in steel girders (untreated steel, distance centre-to-centre being 600 or 1,200 mm), smooth underside. The steel girders have apertures for services. A raised floor is applied over the girders.		Upper storey floors, particularly in office buildings. Cables, ducts and pipes can be fitted in the floor.	Apertures can be made between the steel girders, depending on the floor load dimensions.
	Wooden beams and panels. Wooden beams (max 75 x 275 mm, distance centre-to-centre, 300–600 mm) over which engineered timber boards (chipboard or similar) are placed.	5.40–6 m	Upper storey, roof	Apertures between the beams or with the help of a trimmer construction.

For point-supported slabs spanning a space such as in solid construction there are three main methods of construction (50).

The first method involves perimeter beams supported by the columns. If the floor plan is more or less square, a floor construction can be placed over the beams. The combination of columns and beams provides all-around support comparable to loadbearing perimeter walls.

A second solution is to place the floor types mentioned above directly onto the columns. Instead of a continuous support, there are supports at individual points, which means that the spans cannot be as big as in the case of a continuous support (assuming that loads and floor thickness are equal). Levels of stress will be at their highest at the location of the columns, and the floor edges may also become more distorted than when the edges are supported by a beam or a wall. The extra stress can be compensated by additional reinforcement in the areas of support or – in the case of the space frame – by increasing the diameter of the rods or by using rods of a better quality steel at the supports and along the edges. However, support on individual points always allows for a smaller maximum span than linear support in continous beams or walls around the perimeter. In the case of the third method, a system consisting of parallel longitudinal primary girders and secondary transversal slabs or girders rests on the columns. This system is directional and suits longer, rectangular floor plans.

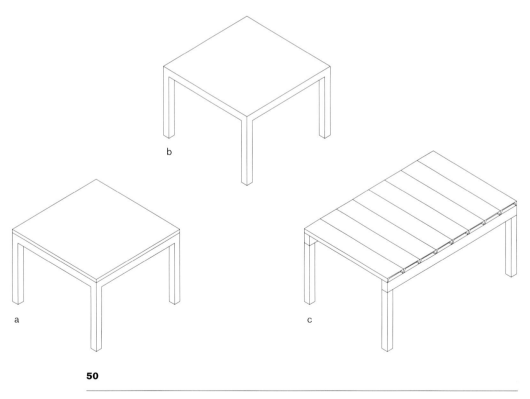

50

Possible span types in the skeleton construction method
The loads from the floor slab are supported by perimeter beams (a), directly by the columns (b)
or a system of primary girders and transversal slabs (c).

Floor openings

The feasibility of apertures in any floor system depends on the composition and build-up of that system (51).

In a non-directional floor system both span directions are in principle equally important. Hence, square stair openings usually provide the most efficient solution as the least amount of slab area has to be cut out and load transfer in two directions is still maintained. The increased tension that occurs around apertures in flat concrete slabs can be compensated by reinforcing the concrete in that area. That is, the slab is reinforced internally without visible effects to its shape. This also applies to filigree slabs and BubbleDeck slabs. However, the area of the opening is limited to a certain maximum depending on the existing stress, load, location and dimensions of the aperture. In the zone around the columns the feasibility of apertures is limited; apertures adjacent to columns may be not feasible at all due to the increased amount of reinforcement in this area (since stress reaches a maximum at points of support). In the case of coffered slabs (52), apertures are generally feasible in the area between the ribs.

If the apertures need to be bigger, some ribs can be left out, provided the ribs around the opening are reinforced. Here, too, the size of the opening is limited to a certain maximum. The thickness of the floor remains the same throughout, which is beneficial for the connection of walls and suspended ceilings. In space frames, openings can be made if stronger rods are placed around the opening (53). Small openings below grid size are not a problem at all.

In directional floor systems, there are structural reasons for making the opening for the stairs in the direction of the span. For example, if the floor is made up of flat rectangular slabs, one of these slabs can be left out to provide a rectangular hole for the stairs. When a floor is formed of linear elements (beams) with a surface of secondary structural importance in between, some of the latter can be removed to leave a hole for the stairs. When a rectangular opening for the stairs is situated at right angles to the direction in which the floor spans the space, a number of beams must be cut away to make room for the stairs. These

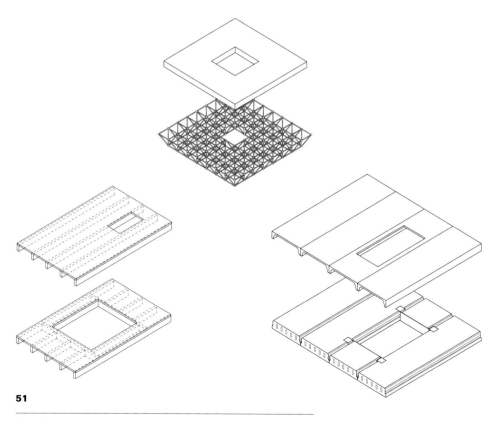

51

Openings in slabs
Openings in non-directional slabs, in prefabricated slabs and in ceiling structures consisting of beams and filled-in compartments

beams (known as tail beams or hammer beams) will have to be supported at the edge of the stairwell by a trimmer, which transfers the load on it to two 'trimmer joists' on either side of the stairwell. These trimmer joists will therefore have to be designed to take heavier loads than the other beams. The wall will also be more heavily loaded at the points where the trimmer joists rest on it.

To prevent the need for making the floor thicker, it may be decided not to make the beams higher, but instead wider, or to double their number. In the case of steel constructions, profiles with thicker steel can be used. (HEB or HEM sections instead of HEA sections).

The situation is much the same with solid concrete floors. Here the extra load can be supported by adding more reinforcement to the concrete. If the stairwell is too long, however, a point is reached where the percentage of reinforcement in the concrete exceeds the maximum permitted level. The floor slab then has to be made thicker. In this case the exception determines the rule which leads to a less economical solution.

In the case of floor slabs consisting of linear girders with infill panels, it is easy to create an opening between the linear ele-

ments, to leave out the filling, and only the area around the newly formed edge requires extra measures for stiffening. If the apertures have to be larger than the distance between the beams, they will have to be shortened by means of a trimmer. The trimmer joists have to bear a greater load and must therefore be designed accordingly. In profiled slabs apertures can only be created on site, while the ribs and a zone on both sides of the ribs cannot be cut. Larger apertures have to be considered at the design stage of the primary system.

Slabs of glue-laminated wood can only be strengthened by making them thicker, or by attaching support rods underneath them. In the first case it is the thickness of the interrupted slab that determines the thickness of the whole floor, and in the second the underside of the floor is not flat, which can prove restrictive for ceiling, walls and cables that are fitted there. If the size of the opening is the same as or larger than the width of the panel, a steel section such as a trimmer strap can be used. In this case, the panels on both sides of the openings must be able to bear the weight of the load on the shortened floor panel. The same method is used with concrete floors made of prefabricated hollow slabs.

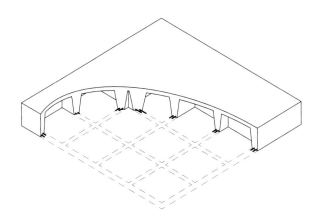

52

Coffered slab
Ceiling with integrated coffers to reduce weight

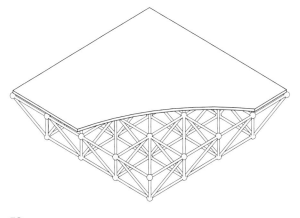

53

Space frames
This spatial lattice frame enables larger spans with slender slabs.
Loads can be transferred to specific nodes.

Vertical constructions

The term 'wall' applies to the vertical surface that separates two rooms or spaces from each other. The wall has a uniform structure and construction typology across its surface. This does not apply to exterior 'façades', which include the façade elements of a building, its interfaces with the outside world, with all their associated (technological, cultural, aesthetic) purposes and the according components (balconies, windows, bay windows, doors, friezes, cornices, gutters).

As has already been mentioned, walls (vertical partition constructions) are subject to both horizontal and vertical loads. The former are caused primarily by wind, but may also be created by attaching other parts of the construction onto the wall, or by mechanical impacts, collisions or similar. With regard to horizontal loads, we will deal here only with those that meet the surface of the wall in a perpendicular angle. Vertical loads are caused by the weight of any parts of the construction that the wall may be supporting, as well as the weight of the wall itself.

There are four types of walls as far as load transfer is concerned (54). They are distinguished, as span constructions, in terms of loadbearing types. Loads can be transferred through a support on one side, to two parallel sides, to four sides, or to four points.

There are also several sub-types within each type. These are theoretical models, as with the classification in three building methods. There are many possible variations and combinations. The variety of solutions is much wider than in the case of floors.

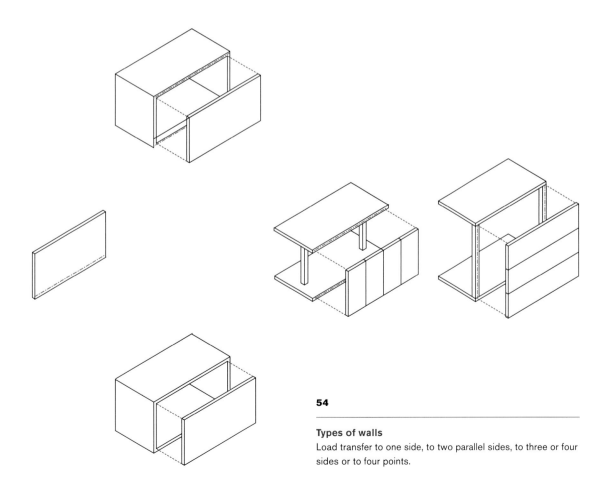

54

Types of walls
Load transfer to one side, to two parallel sides, to three or four sides or to four points.

Free-standing wall

Walls 'stand' on a floor or foundation, which means that the connection between wall and floor can only accept compressive pressure, not tension (55). In order to remain upright, the direction of the resulting force of the horizontal loads (wind) and the vertical loads (dead weight) must fall within the base of the wall (56, 57).

If the wall is unable to accept neither tensile stress, nor therefore bending forces (either because of the material, the foundation soil, or the joints), the mentioned resulting force must additionally fall within the wall's section along its entire height. This method of building walls dates back centuries and is found mostly in walls where stones are stacked on top of each other, sometimes joined using different materials (loam, mortar, cement, glue). They may be of natural stone, tiles made of sun-dried loam or clay, fired stone or sand-lime brick, as well as vitreous stone. Solid walls made of concrete and loam also derive their stability from this mechanism. The great weight of the material contributes to the stability of the wall. The walls can stand in their own right, or be part of a primary or complementary system.

If the wall is part of the primary system, the floor that rests on it contributes to the stability of the wall. The load of the floor causes the resultant force of the horizontal and vertical loads to be directed more vertically to the wall's base.

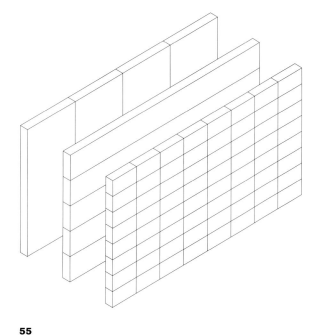

55

Free-standing wall
The wall can consist of panels (with vertical joints), beams (with horizontal joints) or blocks (with horizontal and vertical joints).

56

Stability of a free-standing wall
The resultant force of vertical and horizontal forces must remain within the base of the construction.

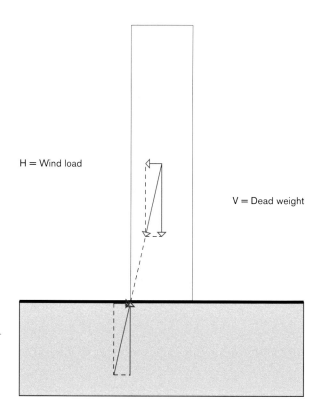

H = Wind load

V = Dead weight

If the wall is part of a non-loadbearing complementary system, the floor slab above does not rest on it – hence, if any mechanical connection is placed between the wall and floor slab it must be designed in such a way that no vertical load is transferred to the wall. The wall must be rigid in its own right as it is not capable to accept bending. In practice, some stone wall types can actually accept a certain degree of tension – and therefore also bending forces. The connection of the wall with the floor above consists of an elastic anchor, allowing the floor to bend and horizontal forces of the wall to be transferred to the floor slab.

The joint pattern can be horizontal, vertical or a combination of the two. In the latter case, the blocks are often laid in an offset bond in order to better spread incidental concentrated horizontal loads over the wall. By changing the shape of the wall in plan and section – for instance building buttresses (58) or an undulated wall – stability can be considerably improved.

57

Swiss Pavilion, World Exhibition EXPO Hanover, Peter Zumthor, 2000
The spring-tensed rods provide the counterreaction that is needed to stabilise the wooden beams that have been stacked loosely on top of each other.

58

Buttresses on a retaining wall
Stabilising the wall by means of buttresses (here they are chamfered according to the distribution of loads).

Restrained wall

The wall is restrained at the base by a slab or foundation (59). Horizontal forces are transferred to the base via bending moments (combination of tension and compression). The materials used must therefore be able to accept tension and compression. Suitable – and commonly used – materials are steel, aluminium, wood and reinforced concrete (60). The wall can be executed without joints, or there may be vertical joints, or it may consist of vertical posts with a secondary infill material.

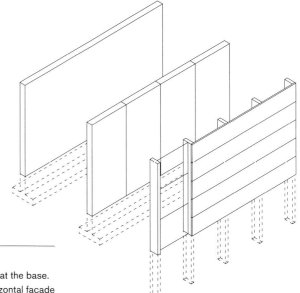

59

Base-restrained wall types
To stabilise the wall against horizontal forces it is restrained at the base. Wall types include solid walls, wall panels or posts with horizontal façade elements.

60

Wind protection at Caland Canal, Netherlands, Maarten Struijs, 1985
Because the concrete screens are curved, they are more stable. They are supposed to shield large ships from strong winds and allow their safe passage through a complex of bridges and locks.

Non-loadbearing wall with two parallel supports

This wall type is always a part of the complementary system and transfers the forces acting on it to the primary system. In most cases this involves floor slabs, and sometimes walls or columns.

In the first case the wall is affixed to two horizontal parallel supports, such as floors or the edge of the roof (61). The wall can hang either from the uppermost floor or rest on the one at the bottom.

In the first case the wall is connected to the top floor with a hinge, and by means of a roller-bearing to the lowermost floor (62). The wall transfers wind loads via bending to the two floors, while vertical loads are passed onto the top floor via tension. Given that the wall is only subject to tension, safety against buckling does not have to be considered – which allows for slimmer profiles. Wood, aluminium and steel are suitable materials because they are reasonably, or indeed very well, capable to accept tension. Reinforced concrete walls are more suitable to accept compression, and therefore they should be connected to the lowermost floor with a hinge. As the wall is also subject to bending (due to the transfer of wind loads to both floor slabs) it still needs to be reinforced, though not to the same extent than if it were suspended from the slab above.

The great advantage of this type is that vertical loads are transferred via axial forces (tension or compression) and not via bending moments, which means that the wall can be dimensioned slimmer. Partly because the distance between floors is generally shorter than that between columns, and because it is favourable to build spans over the shortest distance, this is a very widespread type.

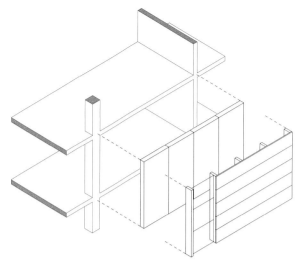

61

Non-loadbearing wall with two horizontal supports
The wall may consist of individual panels or posts with infill elements.

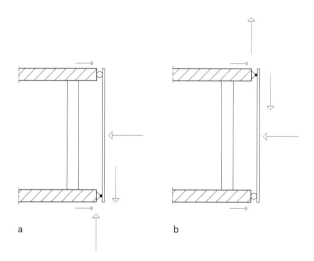

62

Ways for fixing non-supporting walls to the support structure
a Standing: hinge below, roller bearing above
b Hanging: hinge above, roller bearing below

In the second type the load of the wall and the forces being exerted on the wall are transferred to vertical elements – walls or columns – of the primary system (63). From a mechanical point of view this is a logical structure in the event that the distance between the vertical supports is much smaller than that between the floor slabs. A disadvantage is that the horizontal support elements, the horizontal members, transfer vertical loads via a bending moment (and not via axial forces) to the support points. This means constructions are subject to larger deformation and are therefore not as safe (66). If the wall consists of structurally active slabs this disadvantage can be minimised. Often, aesthetic considerations play a decisive role in opting for a vertical or horizontal orientation (64, 65).

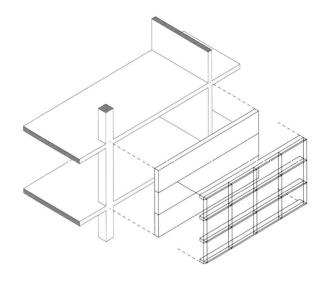

63

Non-loadbearing wall with two vertical supports
The wall may consist of individual panels or posts with infill elements.

64

Muziekgebouw, Amsterdam, 3XN Architects, 2005
The deep horizontal members transfer the wind loads onto the primary columns. They are suspended via tensioned rods.

65

**Carré d'Art, Nîmes, France,
Sir Norman Foster, 1993**
Because the horizontal members transfer the weight of the glass panels and the wind loads to the concrete columns in the façade, they have been designed stronger than the vertical rods.

66

Distortion of façade elements, supported by horizontal members
Due to the weight of the panels the members sag, exerting pressure on the joints between the panels.

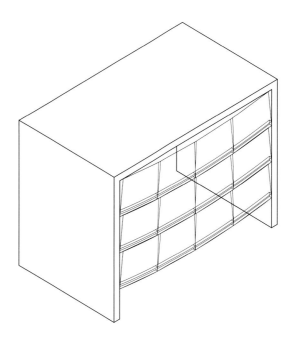

Non-loadbearing wall with support on three or four sides

The loads are transferred both horizontally and vertically. Horizontal wind loads are transferred via horizontal members to the walls. Vertical loads are transferred via suspended rods to the upper floor or via compressed rods to the floor below. The hanging rods only need to cope with tensile stress, resulting in very slim designs with a horizontal rhythm. Vertical rods to the ground floor hampering access to the building are not necessary. In principle the vertical loads can also be transferred to the foundations via compressed rods, but because of the possibility of buckling they will need to be designed to bear a stronger load. Compressed rods cannot be as slim as suspended rods (68).

Non-loadbearing wall with four support points

The wall consists of a slab – or a frame that could be regarded as such – that can accept bending in the direction of and at right angles to its surface (67).

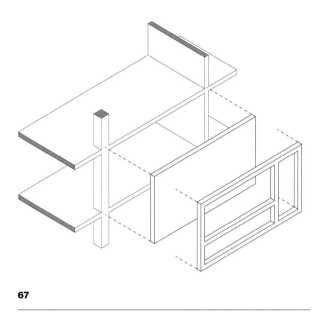

67

Support on four points
Not just slabs, but also rigid frames can be assembled in this way.

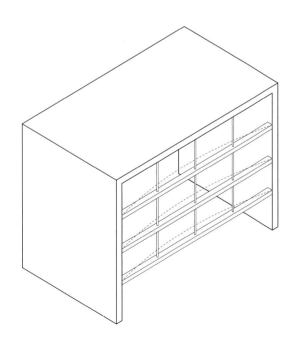

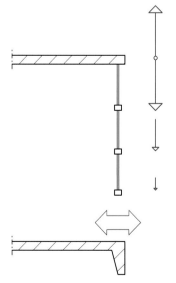

68

Support on three or four sides
Wind loads are transferred to the walls via the horizontal members. Tension-resistant hanging rods prevent the rails from bending.

The loads are transferred via bending forces to the support points which, in order to restrict bending within the floor slabs to a minimum, should preferably be located in the vicinity of the junction of walls/columns and floor. The structure of the wall slab can be homogenous (usually concrete) or be composed of different layers (69).

This wall category encompasses wall slabs or frames within a multi-layered wall with a loadbearing function. Depending on the requirements relating to aesthetics, thermal and acoustic insulation, waterproofing and air-tightness, extra layers can be affixed to or within the framework of the loadbearing layer.

69

Composite façade element
Steel anchors for façade fixing have been inserted into the concrete frame.

Openings in walls

Although in recent decades various buildings have been constructed in which glass forms part of the main loadbearing structure, in the vast majority of cases the openings through which light enters and the outside world can be seen actually represent breaks in the support function of the construction, be it a wall or a roof. With doors, stairwells and open roofs that is always the case.

In principle, there are three possibilities: the perimeter of the opening is smaller than the structural grid; the perimeter is, in parts, the same as the structural grid; the perimeter of the opening exceeds the structural grid.

Openings smaller than structural grid

If the size of the opening is smaller than the modular dimension of the building element, no special constructive measures are required, provided there is a sufficient amount of strong and rigid material around the opening to divert loads (70). Any reinforcement that may be necessary can be made within the limits of the element itself. The façade element has a homogenous structure. As long as the remaining material is or can be made (by reinforcing a concrete element, for example) strong and rigid enough, it is possible to make an opening in the surface. The type of connection between the wall elements and the surrounding construction can be totally different to the connection between the window frame and the wall. The opening is smaller than the distance between two posts (columns or horizontal

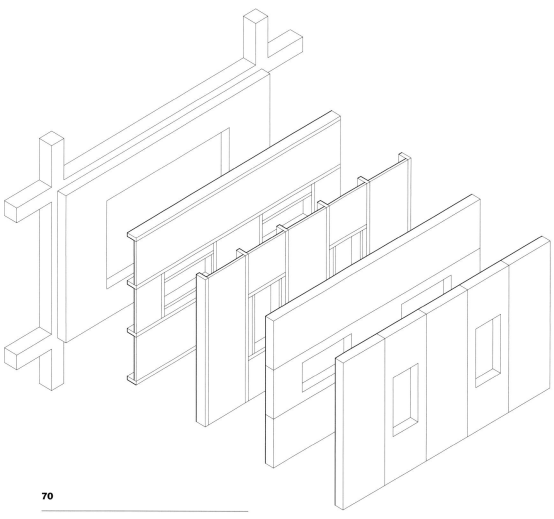

70

Opening in a wall
The openings are smaller than the structural grid.

members) that make up the support structure of the outer wall. In order to connect the window frame with the support elements, a subframe will have to be fitted. The connection between the window frame and the subframe is the same all around the edges. Provided the remaining material is strong and rigid enough, the element into which the opening is cut can continue to fulfil its support function. The connection between the window frame and the wall element can also be of a different type to that between the individual wall elements.

Opening size coincides with structural grid

In a system with loadbearing columns or with horizontal members with infill panels, the filling can be replaced, either partly or completely, by a transparent infill element. The loadbearing structure is not disrupted, so the columns and horizontal members do not have to be strengthened. If the opening runs all the way to the edge of the element, it is a good idea not to break through the edge of the element. This means the connection of the outer wall unit with the next element will then remain of the same type. The connection with the window frame will also remain the same. Different types of connections are often difficult to design and would certainly require extra attention.

For openings with the same size as the structural grid (71), the element in which the openings are made is punctuated so that the loads that are exerted upon it (vertical and horizontal, weight and wind) have to be transferred to the adjacent elements. This means they have to be designed accordingly, and the joints between the elements have not only a sealing function, but also have to be able transfer these loads.

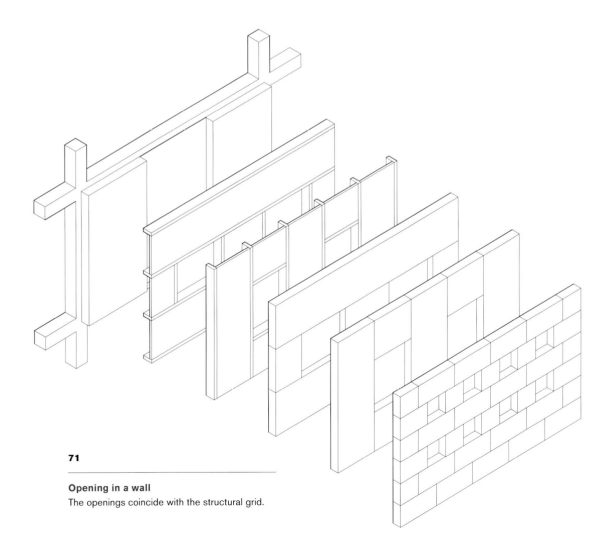

71

Opening in a wall
The openings coincide with the structural grid.

If the opening cuts through the structural posts (columns or horizontal members), a trimmer construction is needed to make up for the disrupted load transfer (73). It may be desirable to double the number of posts or horizontal members or to reconsider the direction of the load transfer.

The remaining material above and below the opening has to transfer the façade loads to the columns or walls. Fitting a subframe around the opening can prevent the weakest link from determining the size of the elements. The connections between the elements should not only have a sealing function, but also be able to transfer loads. The transfer of loads can be arranged via a lintel or a subframe behind the wall elements; alternatively, the connections between the elements should be able to transfer the loads.

The openings in walls consisting of blocks (concrete blocks, bricks etc.) are usually larger than the component blocks. In order to accept the load from the upper part of the construction, lintels made of natural stone or brick, concrete or steel are used. The areas of the wall on either side of the opening must be strong enough to accept the diverted loads (72).

72

Bonnefante Museum, Maastricht, Aldo Rossi, 1995
Lintels are integrated into the brick façade for load transfer.

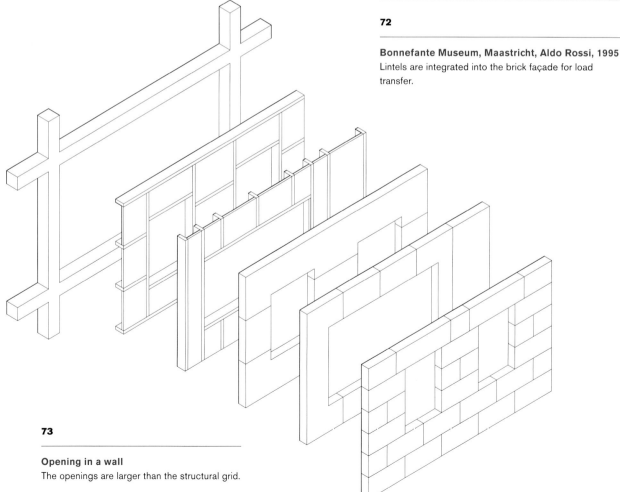

73

Opening in a wall
The openings are larger than the structural grid.

3 | Connections

Buildings consist of parts that fulfil different functions and which have different characteristics. In order to form one entity, the parts have to be connected to each other. Manufacturing options, limitations on transport, manageability on the building site and the characteristics of the materials (especially deformation behaviour) determine the maximum dimensions of the elements and the according requirement to connect them, to join them up. In a connection, a transition is made from one building component with a specific set of functions and characteristics to another, also with its own functions and characteristics. Some functions have to continue from one to the other, while others change. In the case of a window in a wall, for example, both are waterproof, but the function 'to allow light to pass through' changes from one component to the other. If building components have to work together mechanically, then the 'support' function somehow has to be secured in the connection between them. If the separating function of a wall in terms of its permeability cannot be ensured by a connection, then the building is said to 'leak' – thermally, acoustically or in other ways. In constructive connections, building components with different functions and different characteristics are either joined or attached to each other or indeed detached from each other. Designing connections is a matter of 'tying' construction layers with a particular function together wherever necessary, and separating them wherever this is not the case (1).

This could involve attaching layers within the same type of component, for example the connection of a rain-repellent outer wall, through the thermal insulation, to the inner wall; but also the connection between components with different functions and characteristics, such as a wall with a floor or a window in a wall. Looking at the surface from a right angle, these are connections between layers or components with different functions within one two-dimensional plane. Looking along the surface they are linear connections between the surfaces. The connection may be designed by the architect but not necessarily. On the one hand there are conventional, standard solutions when it comes to connections, but on the other the development of connections is the domain of the building industry. In many cases it is not sufficient for the architect to select a connection from a catalogue: instead her or she must design it him/herself. Buildings and building components are often highly specific, both with regard to the technical demands and to the form. The connections between the building components partly determine the technical quality and the design of the building. There are a large number of factors that determine the ultimate design of a connection, and there are many theoretically correct solutions. It is the task of the architect to make choices that do the design fully justice. Connection details are specific to a single building and it is difficult to make generalisations from specific cases. For that reason there are no specific examples in this book. We use principles and models, general knowledge that can be applied to a specific connection in a specific design. Conveying experience in applying these principles cannot be done in this book – that is something that is often only fully developed in actual design practice. However, having the knowledge is a precondition for acquiring such skills.

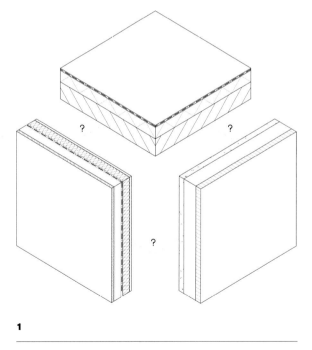

1

Connection of functional layers
Linking functional layers is one of the core tasks of architects.

Internal and external connections

There is a difference between the connections within a more or less homogenous surface or which are part of the same system (internal connections) and those of different types of surfaces that enclose spaces (external connections).

Internal connections

These are connections between the parts that make up a system or type, such as the connection between bricks, the composite parts of a system floor, the parts of a frame and the metal sheets in an outer wall (2–4).

The connection is material-, product- or system-specific and is determined either by tradition (such as the joints in brickwork) or by the supplier of the product or system (such as the connec-

tions between the parts of an aluminium window frame). The involvement of the architect with the design of this type of connection is generally slight as the connection has been developed as far as it is going to be. However, the architect can become involved if he or she believes it to be necessary. One problem here may be the guarantee or the law. Manufacturers often wish to give a guarantee only on connections that they have tested and certified themselves.

3

The implementation of joints in a ribbed floor slab
An internal connection that goes with the floor system.

2

Joint pattern in brick mortar bonds
The form of the joint and the colour of the joint material can both be determined to some degree by the architect.

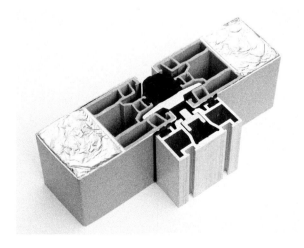

4

Aspect II façade system
Vertical joint in the Aspect II façade system with interfaces to the structural system and the waterproofing layer. (Design: Alan Brookes)

External connections

These are connections between components that are not part of the same system or type. The differences between the components are caused by the specific characteristics of the parts to be joined, whether or not in relation to a transition in function. The connections referred to here include those between a window frame and a wall, a wall and another wall, or a floor with the foundations.

The design of this type of connection is the specific domain of the designer of the building or construction. These are unique connections, specific to a particular building for which they have been developed, or to the architectural language that has become the trademark of the individual architect.

For example in the case of wooden window frames, both the profile of the connection between the posts and the lintels and the method of fitting the glass have been standardised. The industry has developed unique details, partly to be able to provide responsible guarantees on the product. The way in which window frames are placed into walls, on the other hand is typically the domain of the architect. Standard details have also been developed with regard to the connection, although final responsibility for a correct design rests with the architect, who for technical or aesthetic reasons may design his or her own connections (5).

In the connection between building elements, there are joints. Joints are potentially weak points, both with regard to load transfer and the filtering function. The mortar in brickwork, for example, is less waterproof and mechanically weaker than the bricks and determines to a significant degree, thanks to its 24% share of the surface area, the level of water permeability and strength of the wall. Constructions involving joints are expensive, and limiting the length of joints is economically beneficial. The high level of maintenance of joints also plays a role. On the other hand, fewer joints means the size of the elements that need to be connected increases, which requires heavier means of transport as well as cranes. Aesthetic considerations also play an important role if the joints represent a significant aspect of the appearance of the building. It is the task of the designer to ensure that the dimensions of materials and products, aesthetic requirements and technical conditions are properly harmonised (6).

5

**Residential project Hoogte Kadijk, Amsterdam,
Claus en Kaan Architecten, 1998**
The façade as seen from the exterior and the interior:
the position of the frame in the exterior wall largely follows
aesthetic considerations.

6

Panel dimensions in timber skeleton construction
In timber skeleton constructions, the panel dimensions
of floor and wall play a crucial role in dimensioning.
In principle, whole panels are used, on which the
distances between floor beams and wall posts are based.

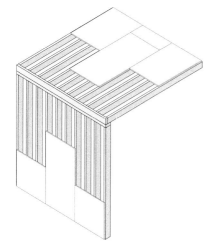

Type and function of connections

Tightness and permeability of a building must also be ensured in the connections. The sealing or indeed permeating function in the connection can be determined by the position of the joints, their size or by the nature of the material used. An overview is given in the illustration below (7).

Combinations of these methods are possible and frequently applied. The choice of type of joint depends on the desired space separation of the construction, the material, the durability and appearance of the joints.

Joints according to positioning of components

The simplest way to provide an effective joint between two composite parts is through the position of the two parts in relation to each other. They do not need to be of a particular form, nor it is necessary to add any third material.

There are three sub-types:

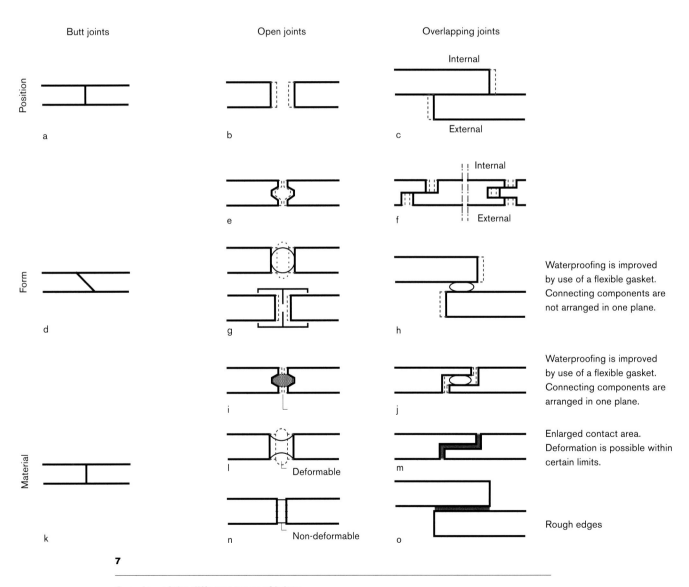

Overview of the different types of joints
There are butt joints, open joints and overlapping joints.

Butt joints

The parts being connected fit very closely together (7a). This is not possible if the parts become deformed through thermal effects, moisture penetration or mechanical loads. Significant tensions can arise that cause the parts being connected to cease to function. The sealing is breached, at least with regard to air and moisture, because the surface roughness of the materials means that the sealing is never absolute. Water can be sucked into the joint through the capillary effect but then has little opportunity to evaporate. If the water then freezes it expands, damaging the construction in the process. Timber constructions with joints of this kind are liable to rot and steel constructions to corrode. These joints are suitable for interior applications (where there is no moisture), for products that can be made to a high degree of accuracy, and which because of the constant ambient conditions do not expand or contract very much. In order to give the parts being connected the room to expand or contract, open joints or overlapping joints can be used.

Open joints

The parts being connected do not touch each other (7b). The open joint may have the function of allowing certain elements (usually air) through, or it may be left open in order to leave room for the parts to expand. Air and water sealing can be left to underlying layers. The interior wall must be completely airtight. The build-up of pressure in the cavity means that the impact of rainfall is limited to the extent that no damage is caused. However, it is necessary to put foil on the thermal insulation layer in the cavity. The function of the outside wall is to provide a first line of rain resistance, to protect against damage to the thermal insulation, to offer protection against UV radiation (which affects plastic foil and thermal insulation) as well as serving an aesthetic purpose. This saves the costs of applying expensive joint sealer (8, 9).

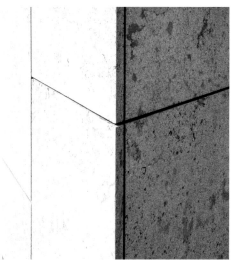

8

Façade cladding with open joints
Chipboard above, natural stone below. Due to the air pressure in the cavity only little water can intrude the joints and expensive waterproofing becomes obsolete.

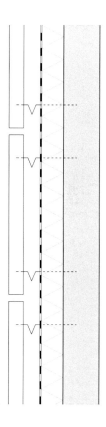

9

Build-up of an exterior wall with open joints
The water-repellent layer should be able to withstand UV radiation, and the anchorage should be of non-corroding material that will not decay. Any water that penetrates should be drained via the bottom of the cavity. The anchor has a draining point to prevent water reaching the inside leaf.

Overlapping joints

This is a very commonly used method (7c). The parts do not need to touch each other – the joint remains open for certain functions, such as air circulation, but closed for others, like rain or prying eyes. If the parts do touch each other, the surface unevenness of the materials will mean that the joint will not be completely sealed. By carefully deciding the position of the attachment agents such as screws or nails, it is possible for pressure to be built up even though the parts being connected can still expand and contract (10, 11). In most cases this connection will be applied horizontally, with the uppermost part covering the lowermost part, creating a rain-resistant (but not waterproof!) joint.

Crossing joints

Tightness has to be maintained even where joints from different directions cross each other. Despite the fact that horizontal and vertical joints may be fitted differently, their effectiveness must never be interrupted.

If vertical and horizontal joints are not positioned in the same plane, this may lead to gaps at the corners (12). This does not merely apply to individual components such as door or window frames but also to exterior walls, roofs and ceiling slabs.

11

Vertical timber cladding of unplaned timber
The narrow slats of wood fix the broader ones.

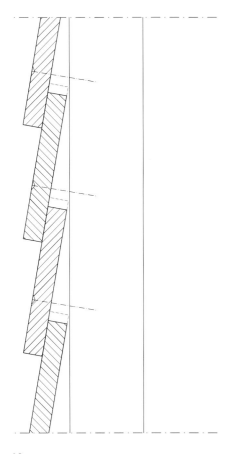

10

Timber weather boarding
Horizontal parts are screwed or nailed onto posts. For each part, one nail is placed in such a way that the underlying part is fixed but can still, to an extent, expand and contract.

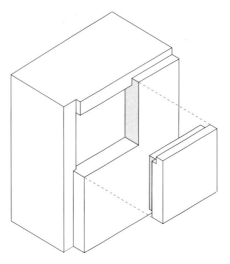

12

Disadvantageous junction of horizontal and vertical joints
The connection in the corner is open in this case; however, it is important especially for airtight connections that they be continuous, with the seals arranged in the same plane.

Direct straight butt joints between hard materials are not airtight (since the abutting sides are never 100% smooth). Hence, the elements have to be joined by means of a third, flexible material, or the two components' materials have to be merged. In many cases, double sealing is applied: the outer seal provides rain-proofing, while an inner seal provides air-tightness. If required, even triple seals can be applied (57). If flexible rubber or plastic gaskets are used, these have to be joined at the junctions of horizontal and vertical seals in an appropriate way. This should be done in a workshop – and not on site – since a workshop provides the best conditions for the manufacture of accurate connections (13).

Joints according to the form of components

In this case the parts being connected possess a particular shape, such as in the case of roof tiles, whose shape drives the overlapping joint arrangement (the direct method), (7e and f). Alternatively, a third element – such as a cover profile – can be added that provides the seal by virtue of its shape (the indirect method), (7g and h). Also a combination of the two is possible (7i, 7j, 14, 15).

14

Waterloo Station, London, Nicholas Grimshaw, 1993
Structural connection and overlapping glazing joint.

13

Corner connection between rubber profiles in an exterior wall component
The connection was made in a workshop. On site, it is difficult to make this kind of airtight seal.

15

Waterloo Station, London, Nicholas Grimshaw, 1993
Glazing detail: overlapping joint with sealant rubber

The open joint (7e) is to a certain degree rain-resistant as a result of the so-called labyrinth effect. Moving air, which contains water, loses velocity in the joint because of a widening or longer route. As a result, the water in the air can trickle downwards. In horizontal joints the moisture has to be led outside via the shape of the joint. In an overlapping joint the connected parts share the same plane, with space being left for expansion and contraction, and they are partly attached to each other (7f). Also, a malleable or unmalleable product can be applied in or over the joint (7g). A compressible jointing compound can improve the seal in an overlapping joint (7h). A big advantage of overlapping joints is the possibility of pressurising the joint or joint material after the element has been put in place. For instance, a prefabricated

wooden outer wall element is attached by means of clamps to the top of a concrete wall, which has been shaped specially for the purpose (16). By turning the bolts, the pressure on the flexible sealing tape between the element and the concrete wall increases, thereby creating a permanent airtight seal (17). If a component is not placed in front of, but in an opening (18a) the seal cannot be achieved with tape as it would have to be applied before the component is placed, during which the tape could then become damaged. This problem can be overcome by placing the component in front of the opening (18b); the better solution, however, is the application of a profiled component (18c), since in this case the component can already be prefixed on site.

Principally, any seal can be achieved on site by using sealants – even at junctions and in corners. However, with a view to life cycle, reliability and accessibility rubber and plastic seals should be given preference (19–22).

16

Fixation of a prefabricated timber façade element
The longholes in the steel braces and the grooves in the wooden element mean that placing the steel brace is not too dependent on dimensions: the position of the element in terms of height and width can be adjusted. Two brackets are used to prevent the transmission of noise via one single bracket.

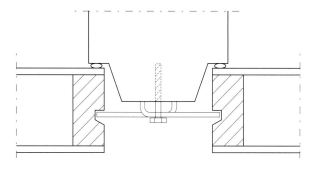

17

Fixation of a timber façade element against the end of a concrete wall
By turning the bolt, the element is pressed against the sealing material.

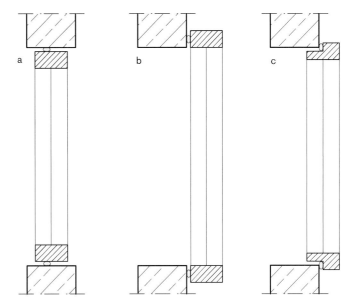

18

Possibilities for placing an element in an opening

a Position vertically adjusted
b Position horizontally adjusted
c Position vertically and horizontally adjusted

The sealing and location in c are optimal.

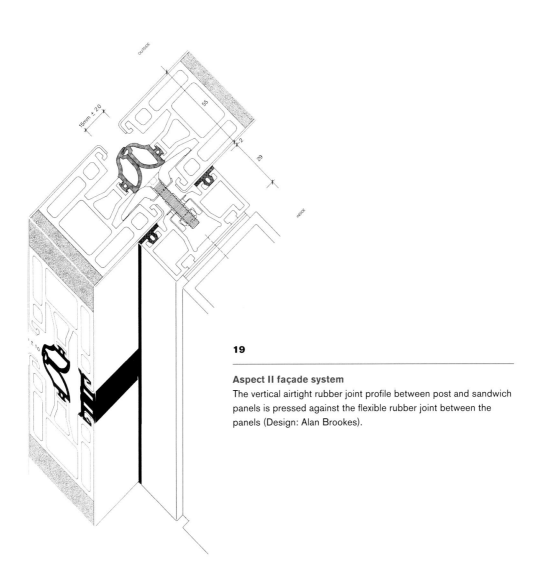

19

Aspect II façade system

The vertical airtight rubber joint profile between post and sandwich panels is pressed against the flexible rubber joint between the panels (Design: Alan Brookes).

20

Airtight sealing between prefabricated concrete elements
Bituminous band is heated and applied over the joints before thermal insulation and façade components are fitted.

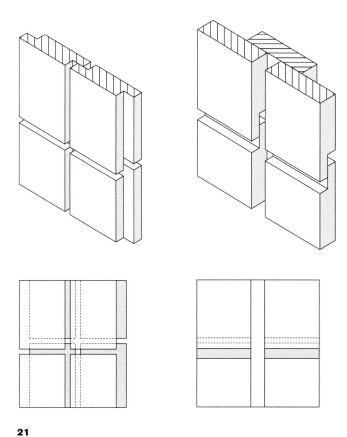

21

Junctions of horizontal and vertical joints
At overlapping joints, gaps are created allowing elements to expand.

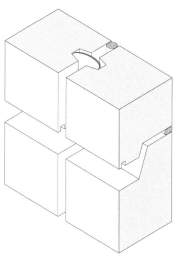

22

Principle of sealing between concrete façade elements.
The sealing for water and air is arranged in two separate layers. The rainwater-seal is arranged in the horizontal joint by an overlap, and in the vertical joint by a widening and a flexible hard plastic profile that is inserted into the joint from above. The airtight seal is arranged on the interior side by means of rubber profiles or other sealants.

Joints according to the material of components

This type of joint relies on the material properties of the components. A physical or chemical connection is created between the elements: either directly (such as by welding of steel parts) or indirectly by using a third material creating the bond between the components (such as in the soldering of metal elements).

A butt joint (7k) is created when two elements are welded together or moulded. There is no room in the joint for expansion or contraction of the materials being connected. If space is left between the elements being connected, it can be filled with a flexible joint compound (sealant) or a solid one, such as cement or lime mortar, as is applied in brickwork (7l, n).

When both connected elements (whether or not they have moulded edges) overlap each other, the surface area for sealing and fixing can be enlarged to allow for better weather proofing and fixation. The malleability depends on the flexibility of the joint compound (7m, o).

Position of connections

Tolerances

The type of joint and required tolerances depend on the major properties of the components to be connected, that is position, dimensions (size and shape) and applied load.

Position

Positioning the building components is in principle a process of pinpoint accuracy. The position and dimensions of the components are related in drawings to a virtual system of lines, comparable to the system of coordinates of longitude and latitude that are used to determine locations on the earth. Both the implementation of the virtual reference system on building sites, and placing the various elements from that system occurs with a certain degree of inaccuracy. The conditions at the building site, the size of the elements and the pressures of time make a high level of accuracy time-consuming and expensive, if not impossible. Also, it is impossible to place an object of a given size into an opening of exactly the same size. Any discrepancy is made up in the joint (23).

23

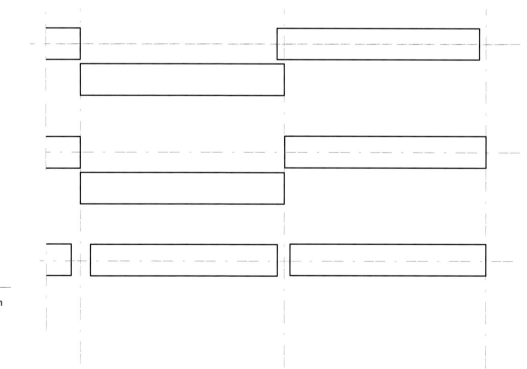

Inaccuracies and difficulties in placing elements
Without sufficient space and tolerances, elements cannot be properly positioned.

Dimensions

The distance between connections is determined in part by the dimensions within which the elements being connected can be made, transported or brought onto the building site. Other factors that may limit the dimensions of building products are the ease with which they can be handled on site, the tools or materials that may be needed to move them (cranes, shuttering, props) and the health and safety regulations at the workplace. Depending on the material and the production methods, materials can be made to an accuracy of tenths of millimetres to several centimetres. Absolute accuracy is impossible. Generally, the level of accuracy increases from the building shell towards the interior fitout. During shell and core construction of in situ concrete structures, dimensional deviations of around 30 mm either way are taken into account. With steel constructions, the degree of accuracy is 5 mm either way. Façade constructions may vary by just a few millimetres. The dimensional deviation should actually be better measured as a percentage of the intended size. Construction components can deviate in terms of length, width and height, but they may also perhaps not be square-shaped (if that is the intention), or they could be flat, curved, crooked or warped. Discrepancies in shape can be accommodated by the joints (24).

Applied loads

Floors, roofs, walls and columns change their form elastically under the influence of increased loads. After the loads have gone, they return to their original shape. The design of the space between connected parts should be such that when deformations occur, certain elements of the construction (including the support construction) are prevented from placing loads onto other elements (including non-supporting parts) for which they are not designed (25, 26).

Furthermore, all materials expand and shrink under the influence of changes in temperature, and many also do so as air moisture levels rise and fall as well. The change in shape is accompanied by significant forces (27).

24

Deformation and tolerances of building components
a   Not rectangular
b   Size discrepancies
c   Warped or twisted
d   Arched
e   Bent
f   Crooked

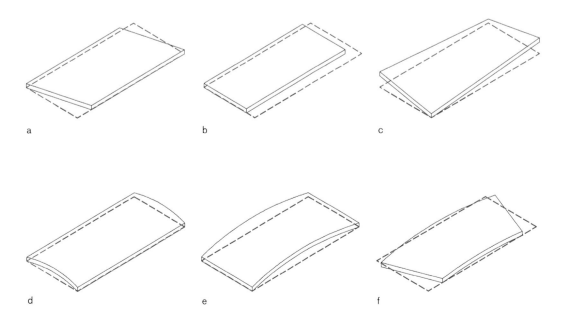

a   b   c

d   e   f

26

Improper connection between primary and complementary system
The bolts that connect the anchor at the end of the beam to the outer wall post have been pulled out as a result of sag in the beam and/or expansion of the outer wall post.

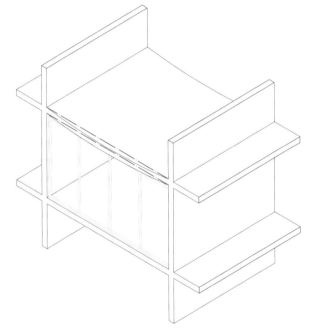

25

Spacing between building components
When supporting parts become distorted under a load, they should not transfer their loads to non-loadbearing components.

27

Brickwork joints
The open joints serve to allow the wall to expand and contract. Although the joints are open, it is not necessary to seal them, because of the pressure in the cavity.

Material-related deviations are accommodated in the joints. Because of the space that is needed to put elements into position, there always remains room (the joint space) which, depending on the desired characteristics of the building component in question, has to be able to fulfil the requirements in terms of tightness and permeability. In order to establish the possible upper and lower limits of the size of the joints, an overall calculation has to be made of the potential discrepancies of the elements in terms of position, dimensions and changes in form. The statistical sum will be less than the numerical total because the chances are very small that all maximum or minimum discrepancies will be reached at the same time. To determine the width of the joint, this size should be added to the minimum size of the joint material. The degree to which the object can expand or contract must never be greater than the deformation capacity of the joint material, otherwise the joint or the attachment holding the construction will give way (28).

Putting up a building does not involve placing the components directly onto or next to each other; room is left for joints. The parts are not assembled in relation to each other but in relation to the virtual reference system. Then, if necessary, the resulting joint is finished with a suitable joint construction.

Adjustment

Adjustment is part of the accurate placing of the components of the construction in relation to the reference system. The position of each product has to be established in six directions, three translation and three rotation directions. Positioning methods and tools are intended to make positioning possible in six directions.

With adjustment, too, there are three methods related to the main characteristics of objects: position, dimensions and material. The method that is used depends on the product that has to be positioned. Positioning is time-consuming and therefore expensive. When many, relatively small elements have to be positioned, simple techniques should be used. The bricklayer lays bricks by hand, using a line strung parallel to the new brickwork as a guide to ensure that each new row of bricks is level. With large and complex outer wall elements, similar adjustment techniques are often used.

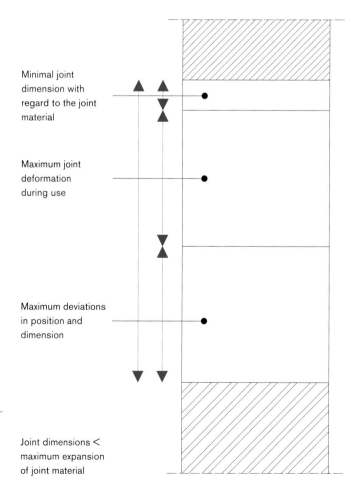

Minimal joint dimension with regard to the joint material

Maximum joint deformation during use

Maximum deviations in position and dimension

Joint dimensions < maximum expansion of joint material

28

Determining the width of the joint
The size of the joint is the statistical sum of location discrepancies, size discrepancies caused by manufacturing defects, and distortions caused by physical phenomena.

Adjusting position during erection

The element can be put directly in the right position if the adjoining parts have been fitted in the correct place. An example of this is the parts of steel support construction. The parts can be manufactured so accurately that once the columns have been correctly positioned, the remaining parts can be attached directly. Another example is that of concrete constructions where the concrete is cast on site. Here, the positioning method is not in the building component or construction itself but in the auxiliary construction (shuttering) of the building component that is to be poured. These objects are also held in the place where they are due to be assembled (by manpower or with the help of a vehicle) and then fixated. The drawback to this method is the necessity of holding the building component while the definitive fixation has not been accomplished. This requires manpower or the use of materials during the whole positioning and fixation process (29).

Adjusting position through the shape of the element

A certain form is ascribed to the product being placed (and possibly to the building component on or to which the product is to be placed) in such a way that when it is finally placed it will settle automatically into its position. In most cases the desired placement accuracy can only be achieved in two directions. Another adjustment method is then needed in order to achieve the desired accuracy in the third dimension.

This positioning method is used for products that are easy to make in the desired form (for example, cast or pressed engineered stone such as gypsum blocks or sand-lime brick). If an extra period of work is needed in order to give the products this extra profile, they will be more expensive. The shaped joints can also transfer loads. A precondition for their application is that the form and counterform can be produced with the same accuracy as is ultimately required in the composite product (30, 31).

29

Adjusting position directly during erection of the element
The prefabricated concrete slabs are lifted to exact right angles by means of the auxiliary construction.

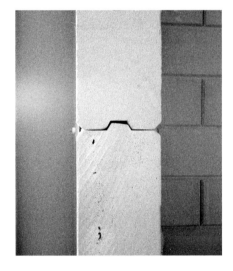

30

Sand-lime brick profile
The positioning notches are tapered so that the stone locks into position automatically.

31

Tongue-and-groove on sand-lime bricks
Positioning notches ensure that the stones can only be placed in one way.

Adjusting position with an auxiliary material

A plastic material is shaped in such a way that it corresponds to the required size. The building element can be pressed into the material, which can still be moulded or placed onto the hardened material. Sometimes the positioning material is also used for fixation and sealing, as is the case for instance with swelling mortar. It is used in adjusting the height of stone constructions (including concrete) and sometimes as support for steel columns. It is cheap, not very accurate and the hardening time means careful planning is needed (32).

Adjusting position with an auxiliary construction

This can be done with standard products or with specially designed products. Examples of standard products are the positioning blocks and sheets of varying thickness that are placed between objects that are to be positioned, for instance tile spacers in tiling work, plastic shims with timber constructions and plastic blocks under the glass panes in window frames (34).

Specially designed products are applied, for example, on large complex façade components for office buildings. The desired high level of accuracy and building speed and the difficult circumstances of the building site (great height) make the extra investment for expensive positioning constructions necessary. In these cases, the positioning constructions are usually already in the right position before the outer wall element is placed and can be affixed. These products are also often used as fixing brackets (33, 35).

32

Cementitious mortar joints in brickwork
The bricks are positioned and fixed, and the connection sealed, with one product and in one single action.

34

Plastic spacers
Positioning sheets that can be slid over a bolt or screw. The thickness is shown by means of a colour.

33

Hoftoren, The Hague,
Kohn Pedersen Fox, 2002
The element can be shifted horizontally to the surface of the façade by means of the anchor rail in the concrete; perpendicular to the surface façade by means of the drill holes with keeper plates; and vertically by means of the adjusting bolts.

35

Kalkriese Museum, Bramsche,
Germany, Gigon + Guyer, 2002
Adjustment brackets for the Corten steel façade panels

Fixation

Roller bearings, hinges and restraints

There are several methods of fixation: firstly, there is a distinction in terms of the mechanical mode of operation. Objects remain in position because the forces being exerted upon them are in balance. As soon as that balance is disturbed, the object starts to move until a new balance has been established. With the exception of parts that are intended to move (turning, sliding), the components that make up a building should not move or rotate in relation to the earth. An object that is not fixed has six degrees of freedom: three translations (in the direction of the x-axis, y-axis and z-axis) and three rotations (around the x-axis, y-axis and z-axis). In mechanics there are three types of connections: the roller bearing, the hinge and the restraint (37). These are almost always

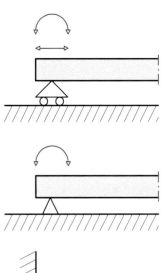

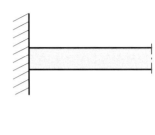

37

Roller bearing, hinge and restraint
The three types of connection in mechanics with their corresponding degrees of freedom.

36

Roller bearings, hinges and restraints
Roller bearings on the top row, hinges in the middle, restraints or rigid connections on the bottom.

considered and designed for flat surfaces – in the other direction, the constructive effect is less clear. The construction element in a roller can rotate and translate in one direction; a hinge can only rotate; and a restraint has the capacity neither to rotate nor translate. The connections between large, loadbearing construction elements are designed as roller bearing, hinge and restraint, and they are recognisable as such (36).

A roller bearing is capable of transferring vertical loads; yet, it can move horizontally – thus allowing material expansion. A restraint can accept a bending moment and is practically fixed. A moment is the product of force and lever arm – the bigger the lever arm, the greater the bending moment that can be accepted (38). With a hinge on the other hand, forces concentrate on one point. Hence, there is a point around which the elements can rotate. In the case of smaller, secondary components the types of connections cannot be classified as clearly into one of these categories.

Fixation through position, form and material

A second way of looking at connections is their relationship with the main characteristics of each object: position, form and material. In practice, these three categories are often combined with each other (39).

Fixation through position

This type of fixation is defined by the position of the individual elements and their arrangement in relation to each other.

The binding power is provided by gravity. The object is fixed only in the direction of gravity. As soon as forces in other directions are exerted on the object, it moves. A drystone wall remains intact primarily due to gravity. The fact that the wall does not fall over as a result of the wind or collisions is due to the frictional resistance (surface unevenness, form and frictional coefficient) of the stones. In the vast majority of cases, additional fixing techniques are used in order to provide resistance against forces other than gravity. The fixation can be improved by laying or stacking objects according to a certain pattern. The method is simple, the objects do not need to be of a particular shape, and no extra tools are required (40).

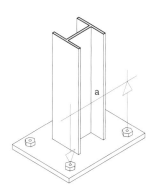

38

Moment, load and lever arm in a restraint connection
The larger the lever arm (distance of the screws from the columns), the larger the bending moment that can be accepted.

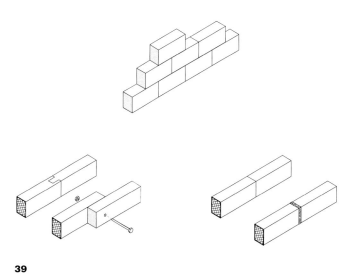

39

Three ways of fixing an object
Fixing through position (stacking), form-locking connections (direct and indirect) and via a connective material (direct and indirect).

Features of fixation through position:
- Easy to disassemble (separable, reusable)
- Easy to assemble
- Secure fixings usually needed in other directions (which may affect disassembly)
- Load transfer occurs directly, no temporary support or auxiliary construction required

Fixation through form

A fixation through form occurs in a positive-locking connection; in that case the object that is to be connected is given a certain shape that positively locks into the other object. Examples include the two halves of a zip, a nut and bolt, plug and socket. The objects being connected do not have to be made of the same material. The objects are designed in such a way that a compressive force and a reaction force can be absorbed in the surface area where the two objects meet, in the direction in which the fixation is supposed to take place. Examples for such connections in buildings are hole and dowel, tongue and groove, bridle joints; they are called form-locking connections. The nature of the material may prove to be a limitation in creating a certain form: not all materials can be made or reshaped in the form that is desired. In principle, positive-locking connections can be disassembled in the direction from which they were assembled.

In the case of positive-locking connections there is therefore usually at least one degree of freedom. For that reason, a material (glue) or an object (pin, bolt, nail) is often added to secure the connection, or the connection itself is reshaped once it is in place so it does not become unfastened (41). The main load transfer takes place mostly through the form-locking connection. The added material or object is then intended to resist any forces that may occur. Anything from small products to whole walls and floors can be fixed by form-locking connections.

There is a difference between direct and indirect form-locking connections. The former is created when two objects directly lock into each other due to their form or shape. The latter is created when two objects indirectly lock into each other with the help of a third, subordinate object. This second type could be classified as an object-based connection.

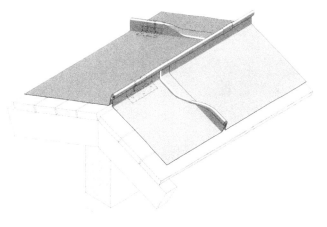

41

Form-locking connection between zinc roof cladding
The sheets are folded on site and are thereafter no longer detachable.

40

Drystone wall
The stones are fixed due to the weight of the stones above. The large stones are on top and lean against each other, giving them greater stability.

Direct form-locking connection: In the case of a direct form-locking connection, the direction in which the load is accepted depends on the form of the connection. The strength of the connection depends on both the strength properties of the material and on the form of the connection (42).

The connection profile can be made at specific points, but in most cases an element will be profiled over the whole length. The connection in that case will have sealing characteristics. One or both of the parts being connected can be given a specific form (43–45).

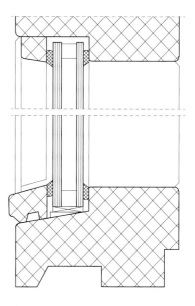

43

Fixing window glazing in a timber frame
The glass is not given a specific form – it is too difficult to form – but it is locked into the counter-form of the frame by glazing bars.

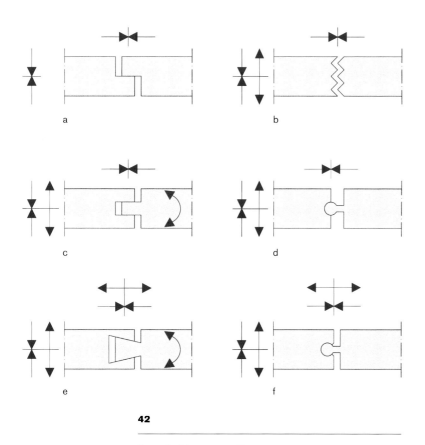

a

b

c

d

e

f

42

Form-locking connections
Several form connections, showing the directions from which loads can be accepted. Connection a can withstand forces in one axial and one lateral direction, b can withstand forces in one axial and two lateral directions; c and d can also absorb rotation resistance; e and f can actually rotate.

44

Form-locking connection in a sheet-pile wall
Although the connection is not completely watertight,
it does have significant sealing characteristics.

45

**Form-locking connection between concrete curb
stones**
Mechanical connection through the shape of the blocks

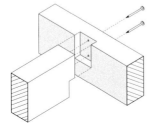 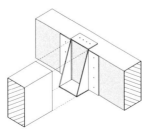

46

Direct and indirect beam connections
In the case of the former, a notch has to be cut into the
beam (possibly on site) with a hammer and chisel; the
metal shoe can be connected with nails to both beams.

Indirect form-locking connection: It is the form of an additional object that creates the connection in the case of object-based connections. This auxiliary tool can be a standard product or be a specially designed and manufactured construction. Standard products are for example rod-shaped objects (like pins, nails, screws and bolts) and metal plates, which may or may not be curved, but which are profiled and have holes, and which are used for example for securing wooden beams together or fixing them to stone components. These anchors are fixed with screws or nails to the beams.

In the case of the rod-shaped elements there is a clear distinction between smooth (pins and nails) and profiled (bolts and screws) rods. The former cannot transfer loads down the length of the connecting agent, and in the case of the latter, the profile causes frictional resistance with the object being connected, so that loads can be transferred lengthwise as well. An important difference between direct and indirect form-locking connections is that in the case of the former, the elements have to pre-shaped to lock into each other, which can be awkward due to the properties of the material. With object-based connections the connecting profile is added to the object that is to be connected with relatively simple means. The additional profile is often of a stronger material, so that the concentration of loads can be absorbed in a single point, such as a hinge connection. This becomes clear in the connections between two wooden beams (46, 47).

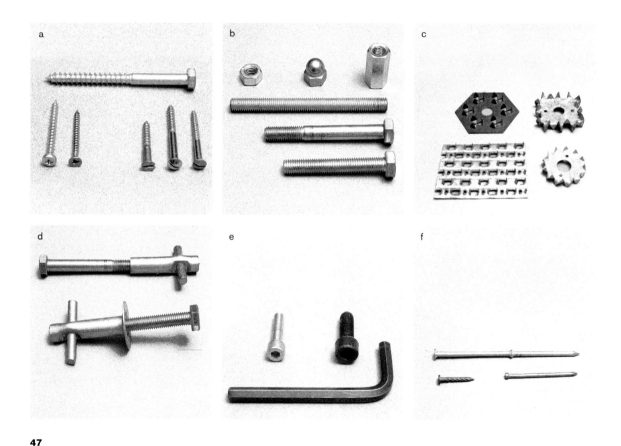

47

A number of connecting agents
a Carriage bolts, chipboard screws, woodscrews
b Nuts, blind nuts, connecting nuts, studs and bolts
c Toothed plates (three types) and nail plate
d Joint fillers which are embedded into concrete, after which a bolt can be attached to it
e Allen bolts and Allen key
f Double nail (for nailing a soft material onto a hard one), twisted nail and a regular thread nail

Fixation through the type of material

In the case of this type of connection, the connection is provided by a physical-chemical bond between the objects being connected: either directly, without the addition of other types of material, or indirectly, with the application of a third material that activates the bond between the two parts.

Direct material connections

Welding:

Both parts being connected are melted and perhaps with the addition of an extra melted material, are brought into contact with each other. After solidifying, there is one material, the characteristics of which may differ slightly at the point of the connection from the original material. This technique can be used with steel, aluminium, stainless steel and thermoplastics, preferably or exclusively in a workshop. Bituminous products, such as track-shaped roof coverings, are welded on site (48).

Casting, moulding:

A shuttering is made around the parts being connected, or indeed the parts themselves form the shuttering. Concrete is poured between the elements, which then sets, creating the connection.

Coating:

Applying thin layers of liquid or plastic material as with cast in situ floors, plasterwork, paint and applying thin metallic layers on glass, for example.

Indirect material connections

Soldering:

Metal parts are connected to each other by allowing another metal with a lower melting point to flow between them. After it has solidified, the connection is complete. Unlike welding, the connecting agent is not the same as the parts being connected, and the connection itself is less strong. This is performed either in the workshop or on site, for example when connecting zinc for gutters and rainwater drains.

Gluing:

A chemical substance is applied between the parts being attached. The glue hardens as a result of a chemical reaction or evaporation of a solvent. With vapour-proof materials, such as metals and glass, only glue that is based on a chemical reaction can be applied, as the vapour of the solvent will not be able to evaporate through the vapour-proof layer.

Glue techniques can be applied to virtually all materials, but the application depends strongly on the materials being connected and the loads to which they will be subjected. The most important applications in the building industry are the gluing of compressed joints in bonds of stone materials, such as sand-lime brick, breeze blocks and tiles; further, glued connections in the interior fitout, with almost every type of material. Glued constructions can be used outside, but the glue connection is then made in the workshop, and the whole glued component is attached with a form-locking connection on site. The quality of a glue connection depends strongly on the right circumstances, and it is very susceptible to errors committed during its execution – which are usually only exposed if or when the connection fails. It is not possible to control this beforehand. The materials being connected can be made sufficiently dry, dust-free and grease-free in the workshop.

Glues are sometimes referred to as sealant, but this is generally only the case when the thickness of the joint being bridged is relatively big (>4 mm) and the material possesses mostly sealing or finishing characteristics, in addition to its adhesive ones.

48

'Welding' strips of roof covering
This technique, which merges two separate courses of bitumen into one homogeneous material, can be regarded as a type of direct material connection.

Cement and lime mortar:

This is in fact also a type of glue – after all, chemical solidification takes place as a result of the reaction of water with cement. The load, especially tension, that a connection of this kind can accept is very low. It is used for stone connections subject to compression and is usually executed on site.

In principle, material connections can accept loads in every direction. In the case of tension and bending moments, the connecting parts and the fixation material have to be able to accept tension. Material connections have more sealing characteristics lengthways (in relation to how they are fitted) than position connections and form-locking connections, but they are more difficult to make, especially on site.

Features of material connections:

- Generally difficult to disassemble (awkward during demolition work, hard to recycle)
- Good sealing qualities when continuously applied, not applied in points
- Relatively expensive
- Fixation over a considerable length is possible, spreading of loads
- Sometimes sensitive to ambient factors; thus welding, soldering and gluing are preferably done in the factory, because adverse factors such as dirt, grease and moisture can be better controlled.

Fixation methods are often combined. Firstly, this is the case when different methods are used for connection in different directions (49).

Secondly, combinations can help to make a connection secure. Where glass panes are glued onto an aluminium frame, it is a requirement that the panes are secured with an object in case the glue joint gives way.

Thirdly, combinations are applied in order to strengthen the effect of one of the methods. This occurs primarily in the combination of a direct form-locking connection and a material connection. The form is then intended to increase the surface on which the fixation is made (50).

When two connection methods are combined with the intention of dividing loads over both connection techniques, it is almost impossible to calculate which part of the load will be accepted by which form of connection; hence, this type of combination should be better avoided. For example, there is basically no point in welding two steel profiles together and then bolting them. It is virtually impossible to work out how much load the weld will bear and how much the bolts. Bolts have to be inserted through holes in the material being connected and therefore always have some clearance. Welding connections are much stiffer. The bolts only come into play once the welding connection has given way.

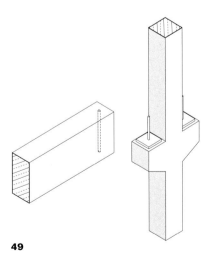

49

Combination of position, form and material connection at a concrete column with consoles
Vertical downward loads are accepted by a position connection, and lateral loads by reinforcement rods protruding from holes in the beam (interlocking connection). The holes are then filled with non-contracting mortar (material connection).

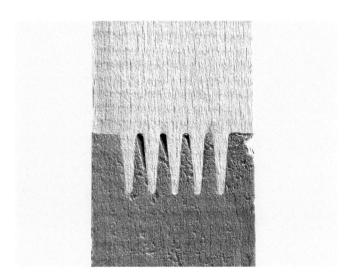

50

Finger-jointed connection
This combination of a form-locking and a material connection is typical of timber constructions. The form is made in order to increase the glue surface area.

Fixation of layers, multiple skins and composite panels

As we have already seen, construction consists of several layers, which themselves can be connected to form multiple skins or composite elements. A construction consists of multiple skins if individual layers are separated by a cavity from each other. The skins or leaves can be linked constructively, but in such a way that one is structurally subordinate to the other – in other words, the forces that are exerted on it are transferred to a loadbearing layer. When a construction is made up of several layers between two spaced exterior skins, such as in sandwich panels, this is called a composite panel. In the case of façade constructions consisting of several leaves, the structurally subordinate leaf may transfer its own weight either directly to the foundations or to the construction behind it. The former is applied to constructions of limited height (up to two or three storeys). Where there are more storeys, they would be too heavy for the load to be borne. Wind load is transferred to the underlying construction via flexible anchors that are capable of absorbing the expansion and contraction of the exterior leaf (51, 52).

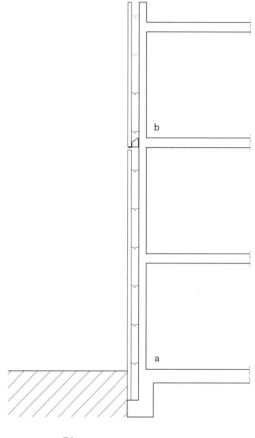

51

Load transfer of wall shells
a Directly to the foundation
b Fixed to every or every second floor slab

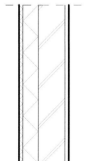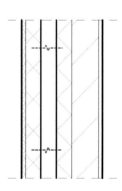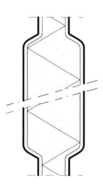

52

Layers, multiple skins and composite panels
In double-skin constructions one leaf is loadbearing, although the non-loadbearing one is connected to it, either transferring wind load and its own weight, or just wind load. In the case of composite panels, the two layers form one constructive entity.

In horizontal constructions, layers can be fixed simply by stacking them on top of each other, if the bottom layer is the supporting layer. Every layer should be able to support the weight of the layers on top of it. In the case of low-load roofs this is not usually a problem, while with roof terraces and roof car parks and so on it is the thermal insulation that is often the weakest link. In cases of this kind, firmer insulation material may be used; or the area where it is possible to walk may be supported by different points on the supporting layer, through the waterproof layer and the thermal insulation. It goes without saying that sealing these points requires a meticulous design and execution, and that this adds considerably to the cost (53).

For loosely applied layers without bond, wind in the form of wind suction has to be taken into consideration, as this may cause the layers to lift up. This can be prevented by using ballast (gravel or tiles), or by fixing the layers at different points with indirect form-locking connections such as screws. Direct form-locking connections are not used in such cases. The layers may also be fixed with the help of direct or indirect material connections. Bituminous waterproof roof coverings, for example, are often fixed to the underlying layer by having their lower layer melted. Glues can be used for connecting layers to each other, either over the whole surface, in a linear fashion or at different points. Layers or leaves are attached to the underside of the supporting layers by means of material connections, for example in the case of paint or layers of plaster. Structural leaves, composite or otherwise, such as suspended ceilings, are attached to the supporting layer via object-based connections.

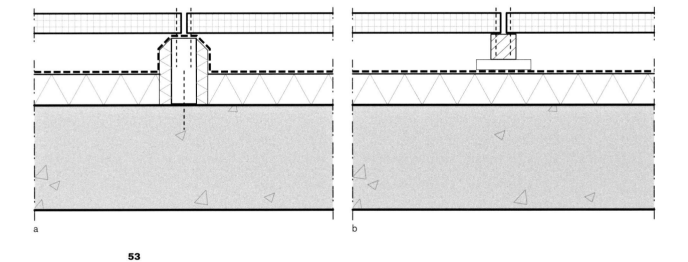

a b

53

Two possible connections of roof claddings
A shows a fixed connection. The waterproof layer runs over the connecting element. Hence, the connection lies above drainage level. In b the roof cladding's dead weight rests on the waterproofing. Water is drained below the plane of connecting elements.

Vertical build-up

In vertical multiple-skin or composite constructions the fixation technique that is used depends on the weight and the strength of the individual layers as well. One of the layers will fulfil the loadbearing function and the others will be fixed to it. In the case of flat roofs, the connection is subject to normal forces. Vertical connections are subject to bending moments and shear, which increase the required use of material. The connections, especially between leaves that are located at a certain distance from each other, are more complex as a result. The layer of material that is situated closest to the supporting layer has to be strong enough to be able to transfer the load of other layers to the supporting layer. If this is not the case, the layer or leaf has to be connected to the supporting layer in another way. This is quite common in practice. For instance, the thermal insulation layer is often placed between a supporting layer and a water- and mechanical impact resistant layer for constructional reasons. The thermal insulation is often mechanically so weak, that other layers (except plasterwork or thin tiles, for example) cannot be fixed onto it. The outermost layer will then have to be connected through the thermal insulation layer with the supporting layer. In many cases this is done with an object-based connection. The greater the distance between the layers, the greater are the bending moments in the connection. The connecting anchor must be designed in such a way that a bending moment can be absorbed. We refer to this as a console (54). The left-turning moment, which is caused by the weight of the outer wall, has to be absorbed by a right-turning moment in the attachment of the console on the supporting layer. The outermost layer should be attached to at least one other point. This is done by means of a flexible connection (mechanically speaking, a roller bearing) to enable tensions resulting from changes in form in the inner and outer leaves to be absorbed.

Thermal bridges: The connection between the two leaves will inevitably puncture the thermal insulation layer. A thermal bridge will be created in the connection between the two construction parts, which could lead to heat loss or condensation problems.

There are a number of possibilities for solving thermal bridges. The heat flow through the thermal bridge is in proportion to the surface area A of the bridge and the thermal conduction coefficient λ and inversely proportional to the length l of the thermal bridge (55). We can reduce the heat flow by reducing the surface area or the thermal conduction coefficient or by increasing the length.

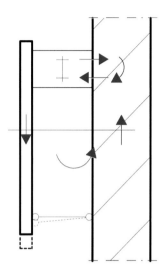

54

Schematic of the mechanical connection between two leaves
The top connection is a restraint, and the bottom one is a moveable joint. The connection is designed to accept bending moments.

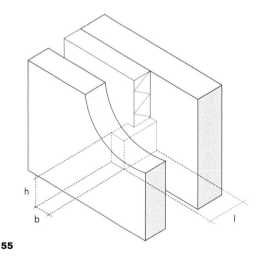

55

Thermal bridge between two leaves in an exterior wall
Making the bridge smaller or using a less thermally conductive material will reduce heat loss.

With the first option, the reduction of the surface area $A = b \cdot h$, the console must be made as small as possible. Assuming that height h is more important than breadth b for strength and rigidity, it is a good idea to keep the h/b ratio as small as possible. In the past, for example, balconies were often connected with the entire length of the floor, but having a connection at just certain points leads to a reduction in the level of heat loss.

Local application of a material with a lower conduction coefficient occurs for example in aluminium window frame profiles, where the innermost and outermost parts are connected by means of a plastic gasket bypassing thermal bridges (57). Whether a plastic element can be used as a thermal barrier depends on the loadbearing capacity of the insulation material.

Increasing the length l of the thermal bridge is not relevant because this is determined by the thickness of the layer of insulation.

Connecting individual leaves: The links between the inner and outer leaves must be made of non-corroding material. Most commonly, stainless steel is used, although aluminium and plastic connections are in principle also possible. The connection with waterproof, thermally insulating and airtight layers must be made with great care, and the use of weather grooves or drip points should prevent water that penetrates through the outside leaf from reaching the inside leaf through adhesion to the connection element (56).

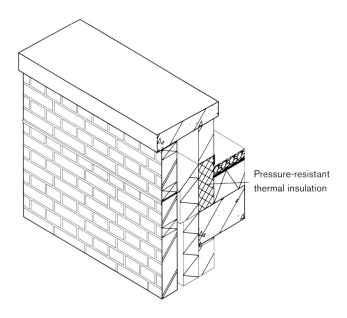

Pressure-resistant
thermal insulation

56

Interception of a thermal bridge in a cellular concrete wall
The interior side of the parapet is made of blocks on a layer of pressure-resistant thermal insulation material. In this case it is cellular concrete, but also foam glass (solidified glass foam) and plastic foams with few pores combine a relatively high thermal insulation value with a relatively high level of strength.

57

Interception of a thermal bridge by use of plastic in an aluminium window frame
The plastic serves to limit heat transmission at the position of the red circles.

There are many possibilities for connections between the inner and outer leaves, for instance via slats, posts and rails, anchors or brackets (58, 59).

The façade elements can be fixed via brackets and profiles (58a). The profiles can be placed at some distance from the supporting layer, so that thermal insulation material can be fitted behind the profiles. The space between the outer wall covering and thermal insulation is ventilated by outside air. Ventilation has to be vertical because the difference in temperature of the outside air and the air in the cavity causes an upward air flow in the cavity. Patches of water or condensation that occur on the inside of the outer wall cladding are transported downwards in the cavity and then outside. Horizontal rails do not offer the possibility of ventilating, and so condensation and the patches of water will remain on the rails. With vertical narrow outer wall coverings it is logical to apply horizontal rails, with the disadvantage of limited ventilation and drainage (58b). With a system of posts and rails, it is possible for the space behind the rails to be ventilated. The rails can be designed to encourage drainage to the outside if the joints in the outer wall covering are open, or inwards if the joints are closed (58d). Large panels are point-fixed (58e). These panels may already be delivered to site with the fixing brackets ready for assembly. Examples include concrete façade elements or a rigid frame with infill panels.

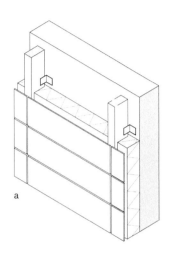

a

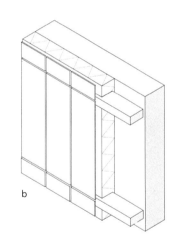

b

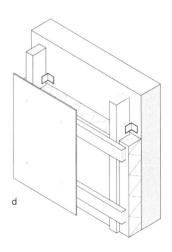

d

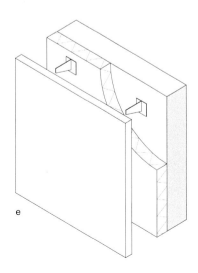

e

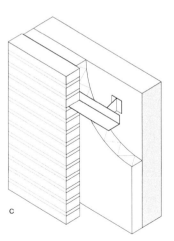

c

58

Different ways of connecting inner and outer leaves of a wall
The fixation of the outer to the inner leaf can be achieved via slats, posts and rails, anchors or brackets.

59

Support console for brick facing
The console is fixed to the concrete slab and acts as a spacer
between inner and outer leaves.

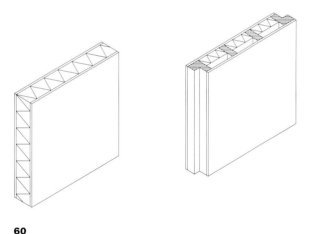

60

Two ways of producing composite panels
The bond can be achieved via the thermal insulation material
or via connecting studs or rails that have been fitted between the
outer shells.

Brickwork facings that are too high – or are placed too high
above ground level – to go directly onto the foundations, are
supported as follows: a horizontal profile (often of L-steel but
also a rectangular concrete beam) that is attached at various
points to the construction behind it using consoles (58c, 59).
The outer brick leaf transfers wind loads to the loadbearing
structure via cavity ties or brackets.

The situation with sloping roofs is not that much different to
that of outside walls. Because water there could reach the thermal insulation, it is necessary to use a water-repellent, but mois-
ture-permeable foil on it. Unhindered upwardly moving ventilation
is required.

Cavities and other hollow spaces should always be ventilated
and protected from invasion by insects, spiders and other small
animals.

In the case of constructions based on composite panels, the
two facing layers have to be connected with each other in such
a way that they form one constructive entity. If these faces are
subject to bending, compressive stress will occur in one face,
while the other will be subject to tensile stress. The material between the two shells has to be able to link them. There are two
common methods (60).

With the first the two shells are connected by a relatively stiff
thermal insulation material, such as artificial foam or cork. The
two layers of the shell are metal layers (steel or aluminium), the
thickness of which is somewhere in the order of tenths of millimetres to 1.5 mm, or thin timber plies or plastic laminates. The
layers are connected by a direct or indirect material connection.
In the first case, plastic foam is inserted into two sheets in a
mould. The foam hardens and binds the shells together. In the
second case the shells are stuck with glue onto hard thermal
insulation sheets. Profiles can be fitted onto the edges in order
to enable connections with another sheet or construction. To
prevent these profiles from forming a thermal bridge between
the inside and outside sheets, they have to have a relatively low
thermal insulation value, as hard plastic and wood do, for example. These sandwich panels are often used in outer wall constructions, roofs and interior applications (interior partitions).

It is also possible to connect the two layers via linear elements. With small elements, they are only fitted along edges, but in the case of larger elements intermediate connections have to be placed in order to enable load transfer between the two shells. The space between the two shells can remain open or can be filled with a thermal insulation material. The edges may be profiled, so that they can fit onto adjacent panels. The sheets are glued onto the profiles. Nails or screws are used on wooden sheets to connect them to the profiles, while the glue is setting. Composite panels of this kind are used in sloping roofs. If the sheets are designed to absorb bending, it is the outermost layers that absorb the compression and tension that occur as a result of the bending. The intermediate material transfers the loads (61, 62).

61

Sandwich panels
The plastic foam creates a structural bond between the two metal sheets. This can only be achieved with lightweight, thin materials since foam is not capable of transferring high loads.

62

Composite prefabricated roof elements made of timber
Inner and outer faces are linked with timber frames.

Forming technologies

The ability to manufacture an object in a particular form determines to a significant degree the application to which it can be put in building constructions. The material of the object plays an important role in determining the form possibilities of the object. In order to be able to design constructions, we have to know how we can shape the composite parts. The most important design and forming techniques are dealt with in brief below.

Basic forming processes

A product is made directly out of a formless material (a powder, liquid or a mixture of the two). This is done by putting the substances in a mould where they set and – possibly under the influence of increased pressure and/or temperature – eventually harden as a result of physical or chemical action. In the construction industry, engineered stone or concrete, metal, plastic or glass are common examples in use.

Stone and ceramics:
Concrete products like pavement kerbs and paving stones, but also walls, floors and stairs are cast in a mould (formwork), where they harden as a result of chemical processes.

Sand-lime brick blocks, for example, are manufactured by compressing lime and sand into a form at a high temperature. Ceramic products like fired clay in the form of roof tiles, bricks, pipes, sinks and toilet bowls are made in moulds and then fired.

Metals:
Steel, iron and aluminium can be cast into a mould. In particular, objects with a non-continuous profile are produced in this way (63).

Plastic:
As is the case with metals, the basic material is cast, sprayed or blasted into a mould. Due to the broad range of available plastics a large number of forming technologies are possible.

Glass:
Glass panes are manufactured by casting molten glass onto a liquid tin base. The liquid tin provides the smooth surface. Glass roof tiles and glass bricks are produced in a casting process.

63

Bracken House, London, Michael Hopkins, 1992
For the renovation of the façade cast steel elements were used.

Remodelling processes

The form of a solid object is changed as a result of forces exerted upon it, without any loss of material.

Forging:

The product is compressed between two tools under exposure to heat.

Rolling:

In a continuous process, the end-product is forced between wheels into a particular form. This is applied to steel construction profiles, and to both flat and profiled metal sheets (64).

Extrusion moulding:

The material is pressed through an opening in a matrix and takes on the counterform of the opening in the matrix. A typical application are profiles made of aluminium or polymers (65).

Bending and folding:

Sheets and profiles are bent or folded between two tools. This application is suitable for steel, aluminium, zinc, copper and polymers (66).

Deep-drawing:

A flat sheet is laid over an opening, before a punch is applied to create the right form. Relatively uncommon in the construction industry, but it is possible to make dual-bend surfaces using this method.

Explosive forming:

A flat metal sheet is placed over a die whereupon an explosive charge is used instead of a punch or press to force the sheet into the form of the die. Expensive and little-used in the construction industry, but it is also possible to make dual-bend surfaces using this method.

Remodelling can be applied to materials with plastic properties (whether or not as a result of an increase in temperature). This includes metal and thermoplastic polymers.

Timber can also be formed at higher temperatures (>175°C), but the degree of forming is too low to be used in practice for creating connections.

64

Rolled steel profiles
Rolled products have the same profile down their entire length,
but extra steel objects can be welded onto them for the purpose of making connections.

65

Extrusion moulding die for the production of aluminium profiles
Liquid aluminium is pressed through the opening and then cooled down.

66

Sheet metal folder
Machine for the bending and folding of metal sheets at an edge

Separation processes

Chipping:
Examples are milling, drilling and grinding. Waste chippings are a by-product of this process.

Sawing:
Waste chippings as well as a useful form result from this process.

Clean separation:
This process, for instance in cutting, results in useful rest material. No waste chippings remain.

Stone:
Stony materials can be altered, but because they are hard, only very hard materials can be used as tools, often a diamond. Since natural stone cannot be reshaped through basic forming or re-modelling processes, this process is the only one that is suitable for natural stone. Concrete, bricks, engineered stone and tiles can be divided without waste chippings by placing notches in them and then breaking them, but the cut itself is not clean.

Metals:
The techniques referred to can generally be applied without difficulty to metals, depending on the type and the dimensions (67).

Polymers:
The techniques referred to can generally be applied without difficulty to polymers, depending on the type and the dimensions.

Glass:
Glass can easily be separated without creating splinters (by making a notch and then breaking it), and drilled, cut and sawn with special machinery.

Wood:
Wood can be easily processed by means of chipping processes and sawing. Veneer is cut from the trunk of a tree (without creating splinters).

67

Sheet metal cutting machine
Much like a huge scissor this machine cuts metal.

Material and connections

Not all connection techniques can be used on every material. Strength and distortion characteristics, elasticity and processability vary from one material to another. Connection techniques have been developed over the course of time for every type of material, and some have since disappeared.

Timber connections

Direct form-locking connections: Material is removed from one or both of the parts being connected so that they can fit together. This is a very old connection technique which is very highly developed in Japan, for example. Families of wood processors often have their own 'secret' series of wood connections which are passed down from one generation to another (68, 70).

The connections are often secured with wooded pins or wedges. Because the form of wood can change substantially under the influence of changes in air moisture, these connections tend to work themselves loose. Another disadvantage of this method is that material is removed from the location where the greatest tensions occur. In addition, these connections are laborious and require a great deal of skill. They are still used in restoration work, but also in the manufacture of wooden frame and window frames, where the form can be made by machines and hence in the workshop (69).

69

Connection of timber parts of a window frame
The connection is glued in the workshop for extra stability.

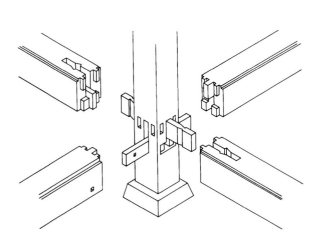

68

Example of a Japanese timber connection
The particular techniques for making timber connection were traditional knowledge carried over within families from generation to generation. Every family had its own catalogue of connections.

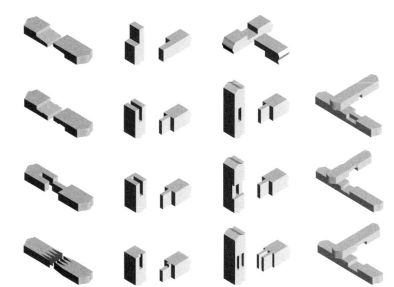

70

Several timber connections
Straight, L-form, T-form and crossing connections

Indirect form-locking connections:
Object-based connection. Wooden elements can be attached to each other or to other materials by means of metal bolts, carriage bolts, screws or nails. Although some material is lost at the location of the connection, this is still much less than is the case with direct form-locking connections. For loadbearing elements, steel support sheets or elements are often used (71).

It is an advantage of direct form-locking timber connections that the direction of the loads can be directed onto one surface. For connections with screws, pins or bolts, the elements are assembled alongside each other, creating moments in the connection, which place extra loads on both the connecting agents and the rods being connected. If the number of rods is doubled, there will be a two-shear connection rather than a one-shear one, making the connection symmetrical (72, 73).

Mont-Cenis Academy, Herne-Sodingen, Germany, Jourda & Perraudin, 1999
Cast steel joints were used in this timber structure.

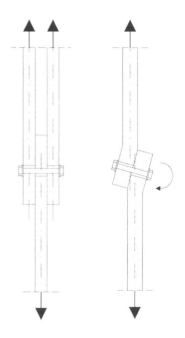

72

Office building Eric Boulanger, Brussels, Philippe Samyn, 1990
Two-shear connection between wooden construction elements

73

One- and two-shear connection between two rods
In the case of two-shear rods, the resulting forces share the same axis, so that no bending moments occur.

Glue connections:

Material connections. These are often used with wood, especially when making wood products from smaller parts. Splinters, chippings, thin layers of veneer and planks can be glued together into sheet- or rod-shaped elements. The latter are used for window frames as well as for support elements. Very large defect-free elements can be made in this way, well in excess of the size of the tree from which they originated. Laminated planks of up to 60 m have been made, while sheets measuring 1,800 × 26,000 × 75 mm can be obtained. Glued connections made on site are not applied very often, with the exception of interior fittings (74).

74

Window frame with finger-jointed, laminated reveal
In this way, wood sections with small dimensions can be combined to form larger pieces.

Steel connections

Bolted and welded connections are used for applications in support constructions. The welding work is not usually carried out on site, for two reasons. The difficulty in controlling every circumstance on a building site limits the speed and quality of production, whereas advanced automated welding equipment can be used in the workshop. Furthermore steel, especially in outdoor applications, has to be galvanised in order to make it sufficiently non-corroding. Galvanisation involves dipping the steel elements into a tub of molten zinc. This means the elements cannot be any larger than the maximum size of the tub. If the component is bigger than the tub, the individual parts have to be connected to each other on site. The presence of the layer of zinc means that the component can no longer be welded. Nevertheless, in exceptional cases, galvanised components are welded on site. This is achieved by leaving ungalvanised the points that need to be welded. After the welding has been completed, these points are treated with a two-component coating. Most connections that are made on site are bolt connections, often combined with direct form-locking connections and position connections. The advantage of this is that the load can be transferred over a larger surface than via the relatively thin bolts and that the component, in the construction phase, can be placed without having to be suspended by a crane for a long time (75).

When thin steel elements are welded there is a high risk that the sheets will become distorted as a result of the high temperatures associated with the welding process. If thin sheets (< 2 mm) have to be fixed, either to each other or to a lower layer of steel or wood, screws, nuts and bolts, or blind rivets are used. The sheets can also be connected in the workshop by means of spot welding.

Concrete connections

Dry and wet connections are used in concrete. Wet connections are material connections that are made on site. The connection is created by casting wet concrete between the parts being assembled. The opening between the parts has to be fitted with shuttering for the purpose, or the two parts themselves can form the shuttering. The reinforcement rods protrude from the elements being connected and are absorbed into the concrete. This type of connection can be made bending moment-resistant (as restraints). The drawbacks to this method are the laborious execution, the need to make and position shuttering, and the time needed for the concrete to set. It is almost impossible to fit shuttering around two prefabricated parts so accurately without any cement water leaking, so if the appearance of the concrete underlies tough aesthetic ambitions this is not the best option.

Dry connections can be made in different ways. In most cases this is done through stacking techniques (position connection), perhaps combined with direct and indirect form-locking connections. This is the preferred method especially where transfer of vertical loads via loadbearing components is involved, but it is also applied in exterior walls (76). In cases where there are less heavy loads, connections can be screwed or bolted with the help of anchors (77).

Furthermore, the elements can be connected via plates welded to the steel reinforcement (78). This method results in stronger connections, but is more laborious in execution.

75

Combination of connection methods between elements in a steel construction
Consoles were added to the top of the column (through welding) by which the girder can transfer its load through a position connection on the column. The bolts protect the girder from lateral loads.

76

State Institute for Archaeological Soil Analysis, Amersfoort, Netherlands, Abel Cahen, 1988
Prefabricated concrete façade elements and columns

77

Bolted connection between two prefabricated concrete wall elements
Anchors are sunk into both parts, which are connected to the reinforcement. After the elements have been positioned, they are connected by means of a galvanised steel sheet and bolts. Due to the longholes, the sheets always fit.

78

Welded connection between two prefabricated concrete wall elements
Steel plates are welded to the reinforcement of the two concrete slabs before casting. On site a steel angle is then welded over the two steel plates.
The recessed connection is later sealed with non-contracting mortar. This connection can transfer more loads than a bolted connection.

Connections between components of different build-up

As has already been mentioned, emphasis in the connection of different layered components is on the connection of those layers with the same function. The composite parts of each layer of material have to be connected in such a way that the relevant functions are not undermined.

Connections within one and the same layer type (such as polystyrene foam insulation) are internal connections that are designed by the supplier of the material (such as sandwich sheets for an outer wall) or are determined very much according to traditional methods. The connections between different layers are the responsibility of the architect, whether the connections are made within the same surface (such as a window frame and the surface of a wall) or on different surfaces (such as where a roof meets an outer wall). Even if the architect does not design those connections him/herself, then at least he/she performs a monitoring function in the process.

When connecting two components with a complex composition, such as layered roof, wall and floor slab constructions with a layered build-up, the designer will always face various aspects that need to be considered. The range of functions, techniques, considerations, available resources (financial or otherwise) – they all to serve to ensure that in practice no single detail is ever alike. In addition, buildings can have highly complex forms, meaning that in any one building there may be dozens or even hundreds of differing connection details to deal with.

In layered constructions, every layer has its own connection typology, relevant to the material that is used. Although the required sealing should in principle be organised for each layer on an individual basis, it is nevertheless a good idea to make the joints stepped in relation to those in layers with a different function.

Waterproofing, air-tightness, soundproofing and fire protection measures should also be ensured in the connection details, while other functions like load transfer and transparency of a wall do not have to be continuous, or in some cases, may even not be legally permissable.

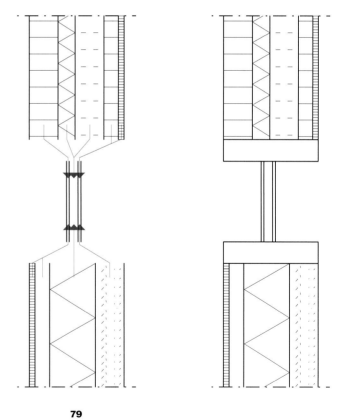

79

Bridging different functions
The window frame is a transitional element between a windowpane with a specific set of functions and a wall with another set of functions.

In the case of daylight openings with double glazing, the functions of rain resistance, thermal insulation, moisture sealing and sound resistance are fulfilled by two glass panes with a thin air cavity layer between them. The surrounding wall may be composed of a large number of layers, all with a different function, and the thickness of which may be considerably different to that of the glass pane. In the connection between the two, there should not only be different types of layers fixed to each other, but it should also be possible to seal the intermediate connection. Meanwhile, the big differences in thickness mean there is a geometric problem. Applying a transitional construction can solve these problems. The transitional construction is a composition of elements – window frames, lintels, dripstones, drainage foil – that is formed on one side in such a way that the glass can be fitted into it, and on the other that it can be joined up with the wall in which the pane is going to be placed. The transitional construction can fulfil all the functions at the same time (to a greater or lesser degree) that the wall is able to (79).

An important aspect of these connection details is that the thermal insulation is placed in one surface, so that it does not have to be diverted. However, if the designer wishes to locate the window frame more towards the outside or inside, the thermal insulation will have to be adjusted accordingly.

Designing a connection

Designing – and learning to design – connections between building constructions is a long-term and complex process, because it involves many aesthetic, functional and technological aspects. It must be stressed at this stage that this is an iterative process that shows similarities with the design process of buildings. Even during the stage of looking for the right solutions, it will be necessary to adjust objectives. Contradictions may occur which will need to be resolved. In this context, the feasibility of assembly or disassembly plays an important role. Standard details are often applied in the building industry, especially the residential building industry, which have been tried and tested over the years and which provide a good technical solution. However, the form of this connection is established in advance and it is the question whether the form corresponds to the design of the building and the concepts and beliefs underpinning it. If this is not the case, the designer will him/herself have to get down to work and find his or her own solutions. Just as much as there is a lack of simple routines for designing a building, the same is true for designing a connection. It is still a matter of 'design', that is finding a formal expression for a specific technical and functional task.

Nevertheless, there are a number of criteria by which a connection can be judged:

Do the parts being connected belong to the primary or complementary system? What function should the building elements fulfil?

What is the build-up of the functional layers (and material layers) of the building parts being connected? Have the layers been arranged in the correct sequence?

Have the functional layers in the connection been placed continuously, and if not, how will potential problems relating to thermal bridges, for example, be resolved?

Can the building parts – with a view to their size and mass – be placed and transported well on site? Do the building parts fit on their intended location ? Is there sufficient room to bring the object in? Can auxiliary constructions be removed afterwards? How will the element be positioned? In all six directions? How will it be fixed? Are the fixing points accessible? How will the joints be sealed?

This chapter explains how the individual components a building consists of can be composed to form an entity. Designers can only make the correct decisions with regard to the layout of the individual components, the openings within and the connections between them if they possess a thorough understanding of the building as a whole. The way spaces are – vertically and horizontally – arranged, separated and connected has a crucial impact on the selection of components and connection types. The way how an entity is composed of its components or how these components are interrelated is called the structure of this entity.

A structure is usually represented by abstract schemes, which may indicate which components are involved, what hierarchic relationship exists between them, how they are arranged and what hierarchic relationship exists between the different arrangements.

Three building methods: spaces and the relations between them

If we aim to enclose a void, to separate it from endless space, we need to create boundaries perpendicular to each other in three directions. When we define the plane of a roof (hence, define the third dimension of the space below) there are ultimately three possibilities concerning the other two dimensions and the way the roof is supported. The vertical elements (walls or columns) may:

1. support the roof on all four sides, thus defining the space under it in two horizontal dimensions and leaving no relationship between the enclosed space and exterior space.

2. support the roof on two parallel sides, thus defining the space under it in only one horizontal dimension and creating a one-dimensional relationship between this space and exterior space.

3. support the roof only by linear elements (columns), so the space under it is not defined in the two horizontal dimensions and has a two-dimensional relationship with exterior space (1, 2).

These three types of construction are called solid or cellular construction method, slab construction or skeleton construction.

1

Three basic building methods and intermediate forms
Solid or cellular construction, slab construction and skeleton construction

2

Solid or cellular construction, slab construction and skeleton construction
The interdependence of space and structure

Primary and complementary systems
enclosing space

Not all parts of a building have to bear equally heavy loads. The choice of certain construction methods allows loads to be concentrated in intentionally selected parts of the structure. The building can then be regarded as divided into a loadbearing 'structure' or 'support' on one side and the 'complementary fittings' on the other. Hence, a construction can be divided into a primary and complementary system. The primary system can be defined as the combination of all primary elements enclosing space. This certainly includes the roof (or the floor slab of the storey above) and those elements supporting the roof. 'Primary system' is not synonymous with 'loadbearing structure'; nor is it an unambiguous concept with the same meaning for every building. What is primary and what is complementary depends on the significance of these two systems in the context of a specific building as a whole. In each of the three building methods, there is a certain relationship between the primary and complementary systems that is characteristic of the building method in question (4).

If the roof plane is supported on all sides so that the space is completely defined in two horizontal dimensions, we cannot automatically deduce that this is architectural space. It is only when we create an opening in one of the walls that we turn the void enclosed by the surrounding surfaces into an interior. The opening creates a relationship between inside and outside: now the inside can be perceived as an interior. On the other hand, the wall is the division between inside and outside; when there is an opening in the wall, the separation is less complete. This spatial dichotomy is also reflected in the structural function. When the wall is loadbearing, making an opening in it will reduce its loadbearing capacity. Where there is no wall, there will be no loadbearing capacity (3). The possibility of making such openings is one of the key features of each building method.

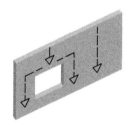

3

Complementary relation of space and construction
The complementary relation of space and a wall construction: where space penetrates the wall (through the opening) load transfer is interrupted.

4

Primary and complementary system
Each of the three construction methods differentiates between primary and complementary fabric enclosing space.

We will now compare various aspects of each building method, including the possibility of making openings and of constructions spanning space. Every building method offers specific possibilities to support a floor slab or roof. For each of the three building methods there are various types of span constructions.

In this context, it becomes clear that the surface that encloses the space in the third dimension, skywards, has an importance for the space that cannot be overestimated. The visible display of forces in the span construction and the role that the walls supporting it have in this context give meaning to the space (5–8).

From a structural point of view, the available bearings for the span construction determine the type of span that is selected. In this context, the most economical construction is generally obtained when all available bearings are exploited. Furthermore, the weight of the roof and all structures resting on it can make the walls supporting it more stable, especially in the case of structures deriving their stability mainly from their own dead weight.

5

Sogn Benedetg Chapel, Sumvitg, Switzerland, Peter Zumthor, 1988
The grid of beams follows the plan and ensures uniform loading to the walls.

6

St. Jeronimo Cathedral, Belem, Portugal, 1514
The form of the vaults follows the forces.

7

Oriente Station, Lisbon, Santiago Calatrava, 1998
The roof construction spans in two directions in a similar way – unlike most other roof structures of railway stations.

8

St. Geneviève Library, Paris, Henri Labrouste, 1851
The elaborate cast iron arches emphasise the longitudinal shape of the plan.

Solid or cellular construction

The space is determined by the walls that enclose it on all sides (9). The roof connects all the walls and is supported by them. Additional stabilisation is not required since the walls brace each other. Generally, the horizontal dimensions of the enclosed space (in plan) are not a great deal apart from each other. There are both spatial and structural reasons for this. In a spatial sense, how we experience the notion of being 'in between' of something or 'inside' depends on the distance between the walls in question (among other factors). When two parallel walls are close together while the other two are far apart, the latter will have less influence on how we experience the 'inside' and will thus only play a minor role in the definition of the space in question. The feeling of 'being enclosed' on all four sides will tend to be weaker in such a space. In a structural sense, the further apart the walls are the more constructional effort will be required to build a roof that connects them. Thus, there will be a tendency to choose the shortest axial span rather than spanning the roof or ceiling in two directions; hence, the two walls furthest apart will lose their significance as part of the primary system. The space is mainly defined by the primary elements enclosing the void rather than by the complementary elements.

Openings

Openings (windows and doors) represent an interruption of the primary structure. The wall is in principle loadbearing over its entire length, so openings should preferably be narrow. In relation, height is not as critical.

Stability

The walls in solid construction provide one another with lateral support, with the dead weight of the floor or roof structure resting on those walls making a major contribution. In principle, no further stabilisation or bracing is required.

Scope for modification or extension

The structure is extended by adding on new cells, where each cell in principle represents a separate spatial unit. Spatial connections between the cells are kept narrow. Modification of the structure involves changes to the primary system and therefore generally requires considerable effort.

Spanning space

In solid structures, all enclosing walls (which all belong to the primary system) support the floor slab and/or roof (10). There is in principle no preferred direction for the roof, which can consist of a non-directional structure or a set of linear elements that transfer loads to the walls due to their geometrical arrangement.

10

Spanning space in solid constructions
Top to bottom: beam grid, radial arrangement, ceiling slab and vault

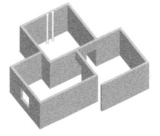

9

Openings in solid constructions
The walls possess a loadbearing function along their entire length. Therefore, openings should be rather narrow; their height is of lesser importance.

Floors and roofs

Apart from already described floor slab types – such as flat, two-way slabs subject to bending or systems consisting of linear girders with infill materials (pp. 41–42) – domes subject to compressive forces or tensile structures can be applied.

When parallel beams or monolithic floors with a well defined direction are used, only two parallel walls of the four walls of the primary system are loaded. The unloaded walls become less important for the primary system. It is easier to make large openings in these walls, since they are not loaded by the floor or roof. On the other hand, the absence of a load on these walls can make them less stable since they are not structurally connected to the floor above them. In massive construction, the unloaded walls play a role in determining the stability of the structure as a whole.

Economic factors

Since all walls have a dual function (support and separation), optimal use is made of the available material in this type of construction. If the most appropriate structure for this type of construction – a two-way slab spanning in two directions – is erected, this can have the additional benefit of enabling thinner construction thicknesses. However, not all materials and building methods are equally suited for two-way span applications.

Examples of solid construction

Gallarus Oratory, County Kerry, Ireland

This early Christian chapel dates back to the 7th or 8th century. It is built from stacked, closely matching stones with open joints. The horizontal joints are slightly tilted outwards to drain away rainwater. This construction is not a barrel vault; the stones are shifted gradually inwards from the bottom up, thus creating a 'corbelled vault' of the kind that was also used for the Mycenaean vaulted tombs in ancient Greece or the south Italian Trulli. The large dead weight of the stones stabilise this structure through gravity. Stones at corners and around openings are larger and more precisely hewn to achieve a more accurate fit and to create a door frame. The chapel was never renovated, yet the construction is in a splendid state (11).

Yurt, Kirgizia

The wall of the tents made and used in Kirgizia and Mongolia can best be regarded as a closed wall supporting the roof on all sides. The continuity of the wall is interrupted at the entrance, and measures have to be taken to ensure that this does not cause the tent to fall apart. A door frame is strapped on to the wall at the place where the construction is interrupted. The wall, which is collapsible, is made of twigs held together with leather straps.

11

Gallarus Oratory, County Kerry, Ireland, 7th–8th century
The vault is created by horizontal stone courses gradually offset to the inside. The walls are leaning in and support each other.

Long leather straps are pulled tight round the top and the middle of the yurt to prevent the wall from collapsing. The upper strap also takes the lateral thrust exerted by the dome on the wall. The ribs of the roof all end on a central ring. It is not possible to support this structure in the middle, but there is no need for this either. This supporting structure is covered with skin, felt or hand-woven textiles in bright colours. Part of the covering can be drawn back in the middle of the roof, to let smoke out or to let fresh air in. The yurt is very stable, even in heavy storms, and needs no guy-lines to keep it in place. It is also a safe structure: if one structural element or connection fails, another one will transfer the load (12, 13).

12

Yurt, Kirgizia
This is a lightweight construction sourced from local materials. The wall is punctured only by a minimum of openings.

13

Yurt, Kirgizia
Drawing of the substructure

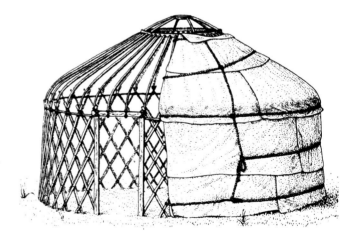

Villa Capra or 'La Rotonda', near Vicenza, Italy

The main volume of this Andrea Palladio building from around 1550 has a square floor plan, and a portico is added on each side. There is a round hall covered by a dome at the centre of the villa. This dome is supported on all sides by the walls of the hall. The pitched roof rests on the wall of the hall at one end and on the exterior wall at the other. The main rooms on the piano nobile have vaulted ceilings that are filled and smoothed on top to give a flat floor surface. The openings in the façade are tall and narrow. All walls support either the floor of the first storey or the roof, or both. This load enhances the stability of the walls. The increase in the thickness of the structure at lower levels can be seen in the cross-section (14, 15).

14

Villa Capra, near Vicenza, Italy, Andrea Palladio, about 1550
Narrow, tall windows are characteristic for a cellular construction.

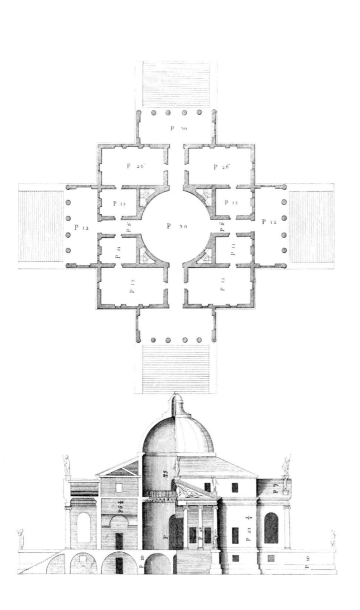

15

Villa Capra, near Vicenza, Italy, Andrea Palladio, about 1550
Floor plan and section-elevation

David Mellor Factory for Cutlery, Derbyshire, UK

The factory from 1990, known as the Round Building, is based on a design by Michael Hopkins and was built on the foundations of an old gasometer. Only the edge of the foundation plate was strong enough to bear the load of the circular wall and the other structures resting on it. The roof consists of radial steel girders resting at the top on an annular support and at the bottom on a masonry wall of rough stone blocks edged with concrete blocks. The masonry is not just a cladding of the loadbearing structure, as is the case in practically all modern buildings, but is itself the loadbearing material. This solution was chosen to bring the building in line with other existing buildings in the Peak District – one of England's most beautiful and most visited National Parks. The wall is interrupted at four points by an opening that is just a little narrower than the distance between the girders, thus making it unnecessary to have a lintel above the opening. The width of the opening is thus determined by the logic of the structure. Prefabricated concrete elements are placed on top of the wall, to give a closer fit between the glass strip situated above the wall and the wall itself and to provide anchorage points – in particular for the supports of the steel girders – which are more easily mounted in concrete than in stone. Heavier con-

crete blocks are used at the support points, to ensure a more even distribution of the load over the masonry. Concrete blocks are also used to edge the openings. They provide a transition between the rough stone blocks and the straight lines of the door frames, which need to rest against a flat surface. In addition, the smooth finish of the concrete blocks means that they are less likely to slip sideways; they also have a higher permissible compressive stress. The circular form of the wall makes for greater stability, especially when it is covered by a sufficiently rigid roof. While the openings do interrupt the pure circular form of the wall as seen in plan view, the curved lines of the wall ensure that sufficient stability is retained (16–18).

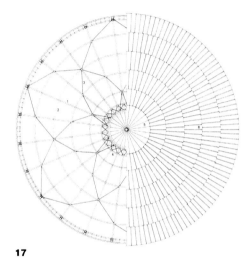

17

David Mellor Factory for Cutlery, Derbyshire, Michael Hopkins, 1990
Roof plan

16

David Mellor Factory for Cutlery, Derbyshire, Michael Hopkins, 1990
Especially the roof construction bears large similarities with a yurt.

18

David Mellor Factory for Cutlery, Derbyshire, Michael Hopkins, 1990
View of the roof structure

First Unitarian Church, Rochester, New York

The nearly square body of the church (1959–1969) is surrounded by a corridor that gives access to a number of blocks of conference rooms, teaching rooms and ancillary spaces. The architect, Louis I. Kahn, considered that the structural subdivision of a building should coincide with the division of the spaces. A person standing in a room should be able to see its structure in its entirety. Therefore, he rejected skeleton constructions subsequently subdivided into smaller spaces since the visitors would no longer be able to experience the structure of the whole. So here major spaces – such as the nave of the church – are given their own ceiling or roof, which make optimal use of the available bearings and are matched to the shape of the space itself. The roof of the church, made of prestressed reinforced concrete, is supported on four sides by the perimeter walls of the nave and by concrete columns in the ambulatory. The wall of the ambulatory is lower than the roof, thus making the columns visible and allowing the whole nave of the church to be seen. The columns could be very slender because they are incorporated in the wall, thus reducing the risk of buckling. The roof is raised at the four corners, forming vertical lanterns for incident, indirect daylight (19–21).

20

**First Unitarian Church, Rochester, New York,
Louis I. Kahn, 1969**
Interior view

19

First Unitarian Church, Rochester, New York, Louis I. Kahn, 1969
Narrow, tall windows are characteristic for cellular construction. Natural light penetrates the interior via roof openings at the four corners.

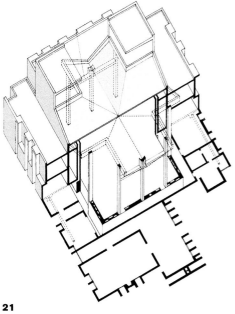

21

**First Unitarian Church, Rochester, New York,
Louis I. Kahn, 1969**
Axonometric view

Luis Barragán House, Luis Barragán, Mexico City

Barragán's houses are characterised by rectangular and square spaces of varying sizes, fitted together like a jigsaw puzzle. The exterior and interior walls are white-washed or painted in bright colours. Window openings are small, to keep out as much sunlight – and therefore heat – as possible. Larger openings are only found at key points such as between the living room and the garden or at the entrance to the garage. Some of the floors consist of heavy wooden beams that span in the most appropriate direction – which can vary from space to space. These beams are covered by wooden floor boards. In other cases, the construction of the soffit cannot be seen; the ceiling is then plastered like the walls (22–24).

22

Luis Barragán House, Luis Barragán, Mexico City, 1948
The large, fully closed wall areas indicate that this residential building was built using the cellular method.

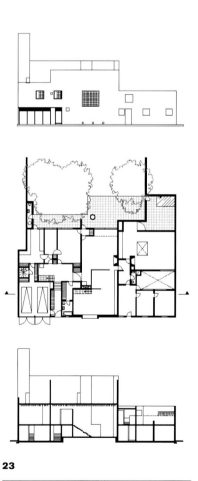

23

Luis Barragán House, Luis Barragán, Mexico City, 1948
Elevation, floor plan and section

24

Luis Barragán House, Luis Barragán, Mexico City, 1948
View of façade facing the street

Slab construction

The space is determined by two opposite walls that form part of the primary system enclosing space (25). The roof is supported by these walls and spans in one direction. The other two walls of the space belong to the complementary system. The primary system does not play a decisive role in determining the design of the complementary walls; the designer thus has considerable freedom in choosing the form of these walls. The space has one dominant direction. This is due on the one hand to the possibility of making openings in the complementary walls that may occupy the entire width – and height – of the space, and on the other to structural and economic considerations. The cost of a roof spanning the space increases exponentially with the width of the space. This means that it is cheaper to place the loadbearing walls as close together as possible, as far as functional and spatial considerations permit this. Or to put this the other way round, the logical and most economical way of spanning a rectangular space is to do so in a single direction (the shortest one). As a result, the short walls lose their structural significance.

Openings

The complementary walls can be omitted or provided with larger or smaller openings as desired, without compromising the structural integrity of the primary system. The openings in the primary system will preferably be kept narrow, but can be elongated to vertical slits extending over the whole height of the storey without compromising the loadbearing capacity of the primary wall.

Stability

The walls of the primary system are stiff across the length, thus providing the necessary stability for the structure in one direction. Special measures will have to be taken to ensure stability in the other direction. These may include increasing the thickness of the primary walls locally or over their entire length or by some form of lateral support for the walls, which may e.g. be provided by (parts of) the complementary system (26). This will result in a hybrid structure.

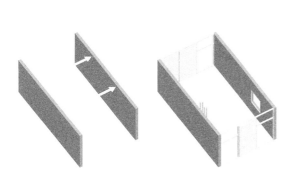
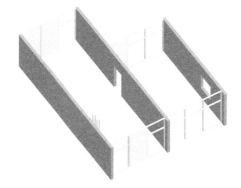

25

Slab construction and openings
The complementary walls can be omitted or penetrated without impact on the primary system. Openings are preferably narrow and full-height.

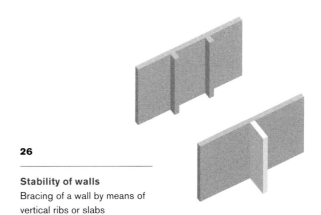

26

Stability of walls
Bracing of a wall by means of vertical ribs or slabs

Scope for modification or extension

This structure can be extended in two ways: by making the slabs longer or by placing additional slabs parallel to the original ones. In the latter case, the openings between the spaces should preferably be kept narrow. Widening the space requires adaptation of the primary system.

Spanning space

In slab constructions, there is always a specific span direction. The roof connects the walls of the primary system, and rests on them. The roof material must always span the space from wall to wall (27–29).

28

Auditorium Niccolò Paganini, Parma, Italy, Renzo Piano, 2001
The direction of the space is reflected by the roof structure.

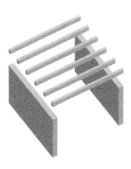

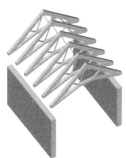

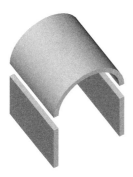

27

Spanning space in slab constructions
Top to bottom: beam grid, girder construction, one-way ceiling slabs and barrel vaults

29

Fondation Maeght, St. Paul de Vence, France, Josep Lluis Sert, 1964
The building possesses a directional structure with integrated openings for daylighting.

Floors and roofs

There are four roof and slab types here:

1. Set of parallel linear elements spaced regularly and interspersed by elements of secondary importance.
2. Rectangular elements in slab form that are arrayed to form the roof (pp. 43–45). These elements may also be vaulted (only on the underside in the case of an accessible roof or slab).
3. Barrel vaults, tunnel roofs or tunnel ceiling formwork
4. Tensile suspended roofs

Flat monolithic floor slabs of in situ concrete are widely used here, especially in housing construction. They offer the possibility of casting services into the floor, and also provide good acoustic insulation thanks to the relatively high weight of the floor. The underside of these floor slabs is so smooth to start with that they require little or no finishing. The main reinforcement in these floors consists of steel bars laid in the direction of the span. The floor can be made loadbearing in two directions by including other bars at right angles to the first. In this case, the end walls must also be considered to be loadbearing; they then also form part of the primary system. The building is then no longer an example for slab construction but for solid construction.

Economic factors

The economic advantage of this type of construction lies mainly in the favourable relationship between floor area and span. This type of construction is chosen if there is no longer any point in laying the roof or upper-storey floor on all four surrounding walls because the span is much shorter in one direction than in the other. The floor area can then be increased by making the building longer without increasing the span.

Examples of slab construction

Mudhif, Southern Iraq

These reed houses consist of arched bundles of reeds placed very close together to form a tunnel-like space. The space between the bundles of reeds is filled with thinner layers of reed. The end façades are made of open-weave reed fabric attached to a number of reed columns, which allow access to daylight and fresh air. It is in principle also possible to have openings in the side façades, but that can only be done incidentally because the longitudinal stability is provided by the layers of reed between the bundles. The form of the reed arches is responsible for the lateral stability (30).

30

Mudhif, Southern Iraq
Interior and exterior view. The complementary end walls permit air and light inside.

Santa Maria de Ripoll, Ripoll, Spain

The church has a nave, two side aisles and a transept. The nave and the transept are surmounted by a barrel vault. The walls of the nave are pierced by openings that are not much wider than the piers left between them, thus preserving the character of the wall.

The historical development of church architecture led to a gradual widening of the openings in these walls while the piers became first simple columns and then compound columns, thus intensifying the spatial relationship between nave and side aisles. At the same time, the barrel vaults turned into cross vaults so that the load of the vault could be transferred more directly to the columns or pillars and allowing larger window openings to be made in the upper part of the wall. The development of this church through the centuries thus shows a gradual transition from a slab construction (Romanesque) to a skeleton construction (Late Gothic) under the influence of growing architectural insights and better building methods.

The termination of the nave by the transept (with an apse and side apses) at one end and the two towers with a portal between them at the other has no influence on the roof, since the vault spans the body of the church from one side wall to the other (31–33).

32

Santa Maria de Ripoll, Ripoll, Spain, 12th–14th century
View of the exterior

31

Santa Maria de Ripoll, Ripoll, Spain, 12th–14th century
View of the interior

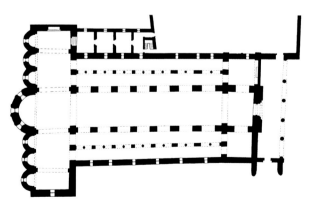

33

Santa Maria de Ripoll, Ripoll, Spain, 12th–14th century
Floor plan

Sainsbury Centre for Visual Arts, Norwich, UK

The longitudinal walls and the roof of this building (1974–1978) consist of a framework built up of trusses 2.40 m wide and 2.40 m apart, clad with panels 2.40 m wide and 1.60 m high. Most of these panels have an aluminium sandwich construction, but some contain glass or ventilation grids. In certain cases, panels twice the usual height are used to permit the inclusion of doors. The end façades consist of large unframed sheets of glass mounted between the end trusses of the building framework. These sheets of glass are backed by glass reinforcement ribs that transfer wind loads to the framework at the top and the ground floor and foundations at the bottom. The required lateral stability is obtained by supporting columns retained in the foundation and the rigid connection between the columns and the joists of the building framework. The 2.40 m depth of the walls and roof is used to house toilets, service ducts and installations. The main hall contains two mezzanine floors, each with its own, independent support structure. Although this building is supported by columns – usually a feature of skeleton constructions – it can clearly be classified as a slab construction with regard of the close spacing of the trusses, as a result of which the side walls represent an almost closed surface in relation to the end façade, and the fact that the building has a pronounced principal direction (34–37).

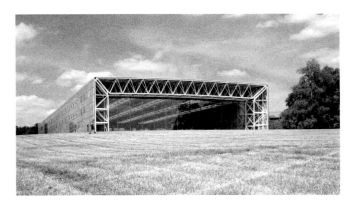

35

Sainsbury Centre for Visual Arts, Norwich, UK, Sir Norman Foster, 1978
The end walls of the building have been designed as transparent as possible.

36

Sainsbury Centre for Visual Arts, Norwich, UK, Sir Norman Foster, 1978
Loadbearing structure

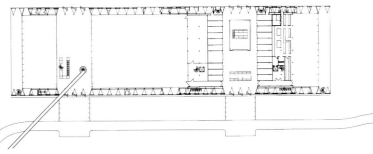

34

Sainsbury Centre for Visual Arts, Norwich, UK, Sir Norman Foster, 1978
Floor plan

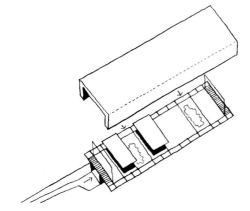

37

Sainsbury Centre for Visual Arts, Norwich, UK, Sir Norman Foster, 1978
Axonometric of building composition

Fondation Beyeler, Riehen, Switzerland

Four walls 130 m long determine the layout of this museum near Basel, designed by Renzo Piano 1992–1997. The roof construction rests on steel-section joists spanning the building from wall to wall. It comprises five layers providing protection from the external climate, each of which transmits light in a different way. In order not to impede the passage of light, no ducts are mounted under the roof. The five above-mentioned layers are: a steel grid, which diffuses the light, a layer of glass that is strong enough to bear the weight of maintenance staff, adjustable Venetian blinds, insulating safety glass and a sun blind consisting of angled enamelled sheets of glass. The exterior longitudinal walls are made of concrete, while the other two long walls and the transverse walls consist of steel columns and intermediate supports clad with plasterboard. The service ducts, piping and electrical wiring, which cannot be mounted above a false ceiling because of the requirement that the roof should be transparent, are housed in the cavity walls instead (38–40).

38

Fondation Beyeler, Riehen, Switzerland, Renzo Piano, 1997
The roof consists of transparent layers supported by steel profiles spanning the wall slabs.

39

Fondation Beyeler, Riehen, Switzerland, Renzo Piano, 1997
The large roof cantilevers prevent harsh contrasting light in the exhibition spaces.

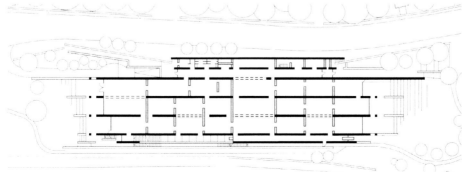

40

Fondation Beyeler, Riehen, Switzerland, Renzo Piano, 1997
Floor plan

Halen Housing Estate, Berne

The slab construction is most widely used for the erection of domestic serial and terrace housing. The wall separating the individual houses must be closed, and must have good acoustic insulation and fire-resistant properties. Heavy masonry or concrete walls can meet these requirements fairly easily and also offer adequate support for floors. A narrow, deep floor plan is to be preferred, as it ensures that the surface area of the façade is small compared with the ground area. It also ensures that the access paths and the utility piping laid under them are relatively short, thus reducing the costs of this part of the work. Depending on the building system chosen, the façade can be kept fairly open except for the need for stability-promoting arrangements in the façade when certain building methods are used. In this project, designed 1955–1961 by Atelier 5, the walls separating the individual dwellings are brick-masonry cavity walls and the floors are of concrete cast in situ. The walls between the loggias and patios of the individual houses are usually of concrete-block masonry but sometimes of concrete cast in situ. The sta-bility in the longitudinal direction of the terraced housing (i.e. at right angles to the party walls) is obtained by making parts of the street façades of masonry. The façades backing on to the gardens and patios are fully glazed (41–44).

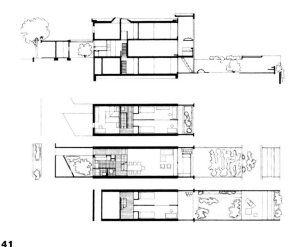

41

Halen Housing Estate, Berne, Atelier 5, 1961
Section and plans

42

Halen Housing Estate, Berne, Atelier 5, 1961
Aerial view of the complex

43

Halen Housing Estate, Berne, Atelier 5, 1961
Exterior view

44

Halen Housing Estate, Berne, Atelier 5, 1961
Interior view

Skeleton construction

In horizontal direction, space is not determined by parts of the primary system (45). The primary system hardly encloses the space (in a horizontal sense), the boundaries between inside and outside are blurred. The complementary system determines the space.

Openings

Openings of equal significance and size may be introduced in all directions.

Stability

Since the primary system has no walls, secondary measures must be taken to ensure stability. This may be achieved by restraining the columns in the foundations, the roof or both (structure without braces) or by supporting the structure with the aid of diagonals or bracing elements belonging to the complementary system.

Scope for modification or extension

The various components of the complementary system can be removed or modified without compromising the integrity of the primary system.

Spanning space

In the skeleton construction, the roof is supported by columns (46–48). The load of the roof can in principle be transferred to the ground in two directions, not along four lines of support as in solid constructions but to four points or even a single point.

Floors and roofs

Apart from the mentioned axial and non-axial systems (p. 47, ill. 44), cross vaults, domes or suspended, tensile roofs may be used.

Economic factors

Vertical loads cannot be transferred directly to the foundations. This must be done via some indirect route, either by the bending of beams or flat plate elements, or via arches. Such types of construction are relatively expensive.

When the skeleton construction is used, a great deal of design effort needs to be invested both in the primary system (stability, diversion of forces) and in the complementary system.

As mentioned above, the skeleton construction gives the designer a lot of freedom, e.g. to allow for future changes in the building. This may make it possible to use the primary system for longer than would otherwise be the case. If however no use is made of this freedom, this is an expensive construction method.

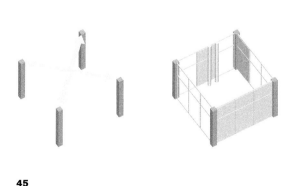

45

Openings in skeleton construction
This type offers great freedom for the introduction of generous openings which can be introduced on all sides.

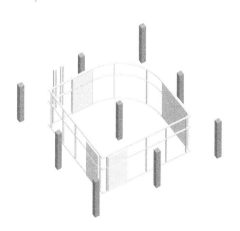

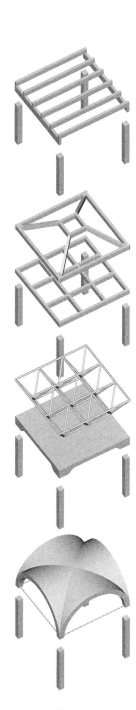

47

Hopkins House, London, Michael Hopkins, 1976
Open floor plans are typical for a skeleton construction

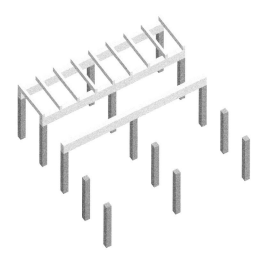

46

Spanning space in skeleton constructions
Top to bottom: Girder construction showing
girder position, grid, space frame, ceiling slab
and cross-vault

48

Skeleton construction
Axial system comprising of tall girders spanning the distance of the largest span
and secondary beams

Examples of skeleton construction

Uma Mbatangu House, Sumba, Indonesia

Traditional wooden houses can be divided into two types. Log huts, made of tree trunks stacked horizontally on top of one another (where the trunks may or may not be worked before being stacked), are found in cold climates. The logs both provide the loadbearing structure of the house and keep out the weather; wood is a fairly good thermal insulator. In hot, moist climates, on the other hand, skeleton constructions are much more common. They consist typically of a framework of columns and beams, filled in with mud, planks, animal skins, bamboo, leaves or reed. These walls are often given an open structure to permit ventilation. Such houses derive their stability from the fact that the supporting columns are dug into the ground. Openings for doors and windows are obtained by leaving out part of the bamboo wall. The roof is formed of a framework of rails, spars and battens covered with leaves (49).

Marika Alderton House, Northern Territory, Australia

Marika Alderton's House and the Uma Mbatangu House in Indonesia were both built in regions with much the same kind of climate: very hot, with dry and wet seasons and frequent (tropical) storms. This house has a skeleton construction based on steel joists. Parts of the wall are made as hatches that can be opened during the daytime for maximum ventilation but are closed at night for security and privacy. Other parts of the façade consist of large sliding doors or latticework shutters that can be raised and secured in an open position. Two different types of measures are taken to protect against possible storms: the whole structure is designed to take heavier loads, and Venturi tubes are mounted in the roof to prevent the build-up of large pressure differences between the air above the roof and that below it. The lateral stability of the primary system is provided by rigid joints at the joist nodes (50), while the longitudinal stability comes from the rigid joints of the longitudinal steel girder with the joist supports, the rigidity of the roof's skin itself and the closed parts of the north-facing façade. The structural nature of the latter com-

49

Uma Mbatangu House, Sumba, Indonesia
Isometric view

50

**Marika Alderton House, Northern Territory, Australia,
Glenn Murcutt, 1994**
The resemblance of this building with the Uma Mbatangu House is apparent: a light construction is clad with a ventilated façade.

ponents is ambiguous: they look like other parts of the complementary system, which could be omitted if so desired, but the
fact that they contribute to the stability of the house means that
they are in fact part of the primary system. When all doors and
shutters are open, the house looks very much like a roof above a
raised floor; the fact that the inner and outer walls are separate
from the roof contributes to this impression. The house was
completely prefabricated in Sydney, transported right across
Australia and assembled in a few weeks (51–53).

51

**Marika Alderton House, Northern Territory,
Australia, Glenn Murcutt, 1994**
Exterior view

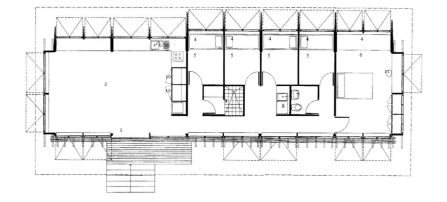

52

**Marika Alderton House, Northern Territory,
Australia, Glenn Murcutt, 1994**
Floor plan

53

**Marika Alderton House, Northern Territory,
Australia, Glenn Murcutt, 1994**
Interior view

Roof of EXPO Pavilion, Hanover

The structure of this EXPO roof by Thomas Herzog consists of ten mushroomed roof modules, each of which is composed of five components: a trunk-like pillar, primary cantilevers with a timber lattice frame, steel joints and a roofing membrane. Every mushroom measures 40 × 40 m. The mushrooms are not structurally connected with each other. The pillars consist of four vertical silver fir members connected by glue-lam Kerto panels. The spacing between the slats of the lattice frame follows the trajectory of forces in the roof. Since the roof modules are structurally independent from each other, the building could theoretically be extended in all directions. The building was erected using the additive building method (54–57).

54

Roof of EXPO Pavilion, Hanover, Thomas Herzog, 2000
Exterior view

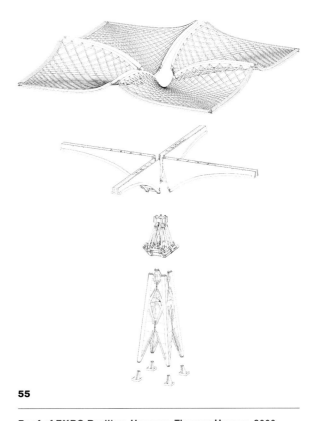

55

Roof of EXPO Pavilion, Hanover, Thomas Herzog, 2000
Components of a mushroom roof module

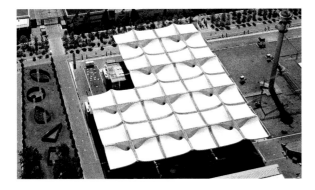

56

Roof of EXPO Pavilion, Hanover, Thomas Herzog, 2000
The roof consists of ten similar, independent mushroom-like modules.

57

Roof of EXPO Pavilion, Hanover, Thomas Herzog, 2000
Connection of cap and stem

Renault Distribution Centre, Swindon, UK

This building by Sir Norman Foster, erected 1980–1982, offers 20,000 m² of storage space and 4,000 m² of office space. The primary system consists of steel columns on a 24 × 24 m grid that are connected by bent steel girders, part of the weight of which is taken up by cables from the top of the columns. Smaller steel girders, also partially supported, are arranged in a triangular pattern between the main girders. The roof is covered with profiled steel sheeting, arranged in such a way as to give a uniform load distribution over the whole structure. The exterior walls form part of the complementary system. Their connection with the main structure permits relatively large movements of the roof. Some parts of the exterior walls are fully glazed, while other parts consist of sandwich panels.

The structure gets its stability from the columns restrained in the foundations and the connections between the columns and the main roof girders. These connections are stiffened by the tie-bars joining the columns and the girders, forming an acute angle with the former. The girder, the column and the tie-bars form two rigid triangles. The building is extendible in all directions without the need for major modifications to the structure (58–61).

59

Renault Distribution Centre, Swindon, UK,
Sir Norman Foster, 1982
The arrangement of the roof elements creates homogenous loading onto columns and primary girders.

58

Renault Distribution Centre, Swindon, UK,
Sir Norman Foster, 1982
Exterior view

60

Renault Distribution Centre, Swindon, UK,
Sir Norman Foster, 1982
Steel columns are connected by bent steel girders.

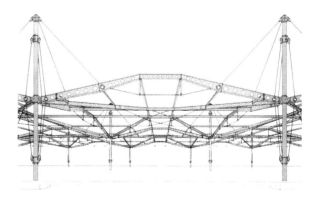

61

Renault Distribution Centre, Swindon, UK,
Sir Norman Foster, 1982
Structural system

TWA Terminal Building, New York

The four concrete shells forming the roof of the main building (1956–1962, Eero Saarinen) are supported by four gigantic double columns. Each shell is more or less diamond-shaped in plan view, with bent edges, and is supported by columns under two diametrically opposed points on its surface. This support system would leave the shells in unstable equilibrium were it not for the fact that all four shells touch at a common point. Thus, the roof structure is of the integral type: all four roof elements play an important role in the formation of the finished structure. The gaps between the shells are glazed. The façades of the main building are all fully glazed and do not form part of the primary system. The spatial possibilities offered by the skeleton construction are used to position the entrance on one side of the building and the access to the boarding zone diametrically opposite. On this main axis between entrance and boarding, two low-rise subordinate buildings are sheltered under the wings of the main building. There is no structural connection between them and the shell construction of the roof (62–65).

62

**TWA Terminal, New York,
Eero Saarinen, 1962**
Night view of the building

63

**TWA Terminal, New York,
Eero Saarinen, 1962**
Aerial view. The joints between the shells are clearly visible.

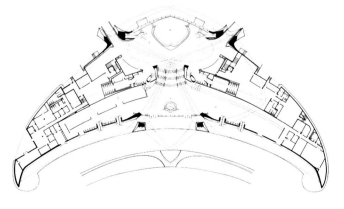

64

**TWA Terminal, New York,
Eero Saarinen, 1962**
Exterior view

65

**TWA Terminal, New York,
Eero Saarinen, 1962**
Floor plan

To some extent, the described building methods are theoretical models. Real buildings are richer and more complex than these models, but the archetypes described above – or combinations and variants of them – may be recognised in many buildings. Even if the plan view of a building is not square but round, the slabs are not parallel or the columns are not situated on the nodes of a square grid, the buildings can still display the basic characteristics of the solid, slab or skeleton construction. It is often a question of proportion: a row of closely spaced columns can be regarded as a slab if the distance to the next row is large enough. Many buildings display combinations of different constructional styles, both in a horizontal and in a vertical direction. Horizontal combinations may be found (for example) when columns are used inside a solid structure to create more space, or conversely when a colonnade or portico is added on the outside of a solid building to create greater involvement with the environment. One commonly occurring vertical combination is that of a skeleton construction at ground level and a solid or slab construction on top.

Horizontal relations between spaces

Buildings rarely consist of a single space but rather a series of spaces next to and often also above of each other. The creation and arrangement of multiple spaces in a building can be realised in various ways.

Division of space

Within the primary unit, complementary elements can be used to divide the main space into smaller parts (69). The partition used for this purpose does not belong to the primary system. This case embodies a certain internal contradiction: the construction spans the whole module of the primary system, while in a given room only the divided module is visible. It may be asked whether it is worth taking the trouble to achieve this large span if the result cannot be experienced after all (66, 67). One reason for this open plan division of floor space is the higher flexibility in the event of a change in use of the building. Then it may no longer be desirable to divide the space, or it may be desirable to divide it up in a different way.

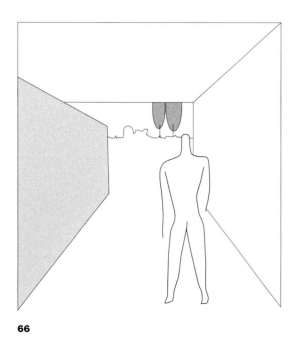

66

Division of space
It is possible to extend the partitions not up to the height of the roof or ceiling, thus exposing the full scope of the span.

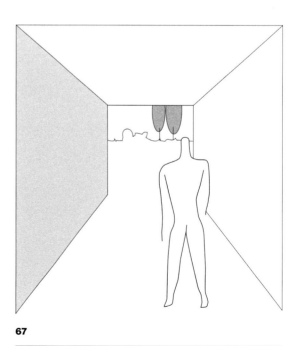

67

Multiplication of space
If space is repeated in an array of similar rooms, the partitions typically reach full height and one only has a sense of the individual space.

It may also be desirable to have a larger number of smaller rooms on upper floors in a multi-storey building. In order to keep construction cost at bay, it makes sense to place vertical loadbearing elements on top of each other wherever possible, and not on a horizontal element (such as floor slabs or beams). This means that the large span will be maintained on the upper floors, the space being divided further with the aid of complementary elements. Such an approach should however be used with care. Every floor structure is subject to deflection, no matter how slightly. If the partition wall is structurally affected by this deflection, it may become a loadbearing element belonging to the primary system (68).

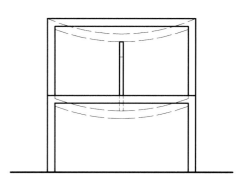

68

Complementary walls
If complementary partitions are erected, deflection of roof and soffit has to be taken into account so that the partition does not act as a primary wall.

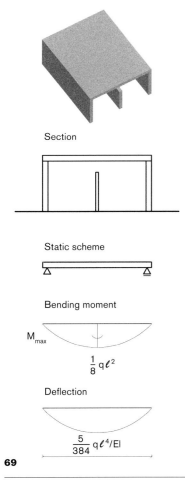

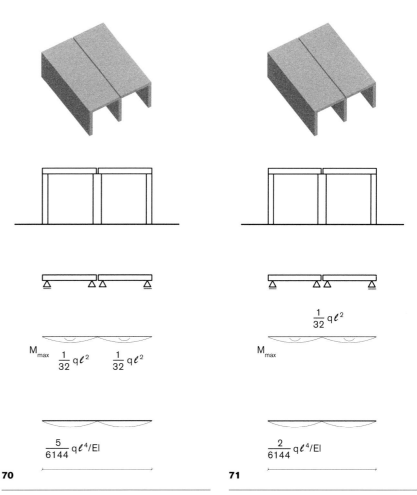

Section

Static scheme

Bending moment

M_{max}

$$\frac{1}{8} q\ell^2$$

M_{max} $\quad \frac{1}{32} q\ell^2 \quad \frac{1}{32} q\ell^2$

$$\frac{1}{32} q\ell^2$$

M_{max}

Deflection

$$\frac{5}{384} q\ell^4/EI$$

$$\frac{5}{6144} q\ell^4/EI$$

$$\frac{2}{6144} q\ell^4/EI$$

69

70

71

Division of space
The partition is not part of the primary structure and must not be structurally connected to the roof.

Additive multiplication of space
The roof is divided along the partition and consists of several, independent parts.

Integral multiplication of space
The roof continues across the partition (continuous beam). The deflection and loading of the one half has an impact on the other half. However, the overall deflection is lower.

This gives rise to another internal contradiction: the wall that is intended as part of the complementary system has suddenly become part of the primary system. Building components that were not meant to be loadbearing might possibly fail under such changed conditions. Complex sliding or elastic connections need to be used to deal with such situations. This issue is related to the connection of complementary façade systems to the primary structure.

Multiplication of space

In addition, multiple spaces can be created in a building by joining primary units together (70, 71). Such sequences of spaces can be spanned in two different ways: using the additive and the integral method (Heinz Ronner et. al., *Baustruktur*, 1995).

In the additive method, each space in a sequence is spanned by a separate floor or roof (70, 72). Where the spans meet, they are 'cut in two' in a structural sense. In principle, the support structure is doubled at the points where two spaces meet. Where the four unit cells of a skeleton construction meet, there will be four columns. Since if we assume that each column supporting a given cell is dimensioned as economically as possible for maximum load, then the point of support will be quadrupled where four cells meet. These four separate columns do not form a joint structural unit.

Examples of the additive method are the Richards Medical Research Laboratories in Philadelphia designed by Louis I. Kahn in 1961 (73) and the Town Hall in Ter Aar near Leiden in the Netherlands, designed by Joop van Stigt in 1965 (74, 75).

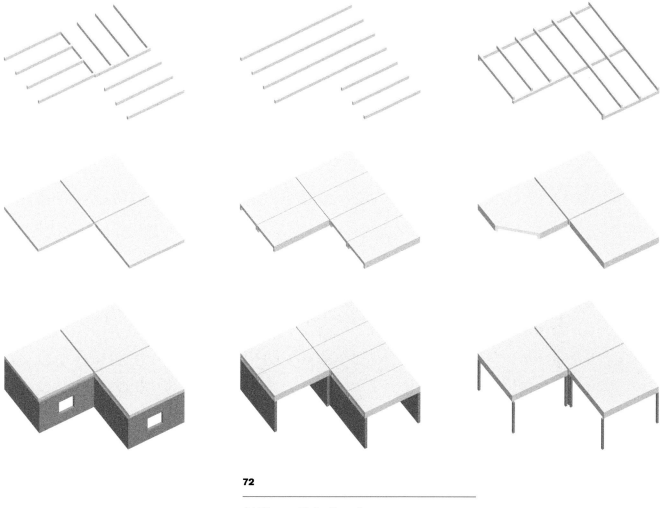

72

Additive multiplication of space
Individual units are added to form a building.

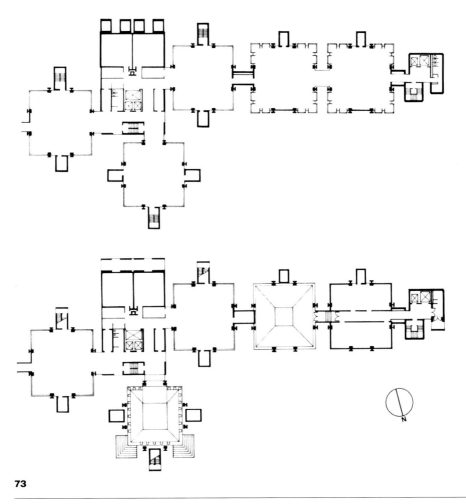

73

Richards Medical Research Laboratories, Philadelphia, Louis I. Kahn, 1962
The building consists of a number of structural units that are clearly expressed in plan.

74

Ter Aar Town Hall, Netherlands, Joop van Stigt, 1965
This building is an example for the additive multiplication of space.

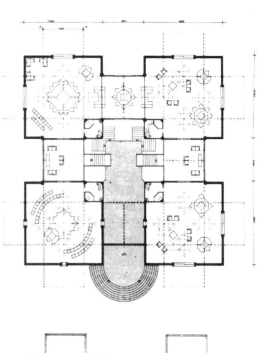

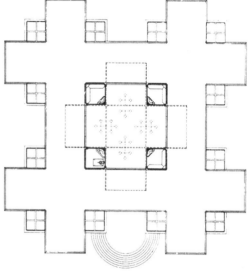

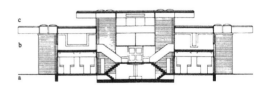

75

**Ter Aar Town Hall, Netherlands,
Joop van Stigt, 1965**
Floor plans and cross section

Integral multiplication of space

In the integral method, floor slabs (or roofs) continue over several spaces without interruption (76). In solid constructions and skeleton constructions with non-axial floor systems, this occurs in two directions, while in slab constructions it occurs in one. A negative bending moment is produced at the point of support, which reduces the deflection of the floor (71). This means that the floor slab can be thinner. The presence of a cantilever reinforces this favourable effect. It may thus be concluded that floor constructions based on the integral method are in principle more economical.

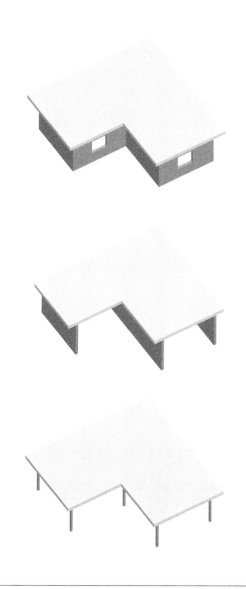

76

Integral multiplication of space
The whole building can be regarded as one structural unit.

Connection of space

If we cannot enter a space or cannot see it because no light falls into it, it cannot really be called a space in an architectural sense. Accessibility and perceptibility are essential characteristics of space. The possibilities of making openings in walls or roofs to ensure accessibility and perceptibility determine the nature of the building methods discussed above. We will now consider some implications of this point in greater detail.

There is a basic difference between the walls of the primary and complementary systems with regard to the scope for making openings in them (77). In a wall of the complementary system, the weight of the material above the opening is borne by the material on both sides of the opening. In a wall of the primary system, not only the weight of the portion of wall above the opening but also the load derived from the floor or roof structure resting on it must be transferred round the opening to the foundations. The portion of wall above the opening thus plays a structural role in the primary system. As a result, openings in the primary system should preferably be kept narrow. The narrower the opening, the lower the load that has to be diverted and the larger the portions of wall that can transfer this load to the foundations. The width of openings in walls of the complementary system is much less of a problem, especially if such an opening extends right up to the next floor slab (79).

One way of creating openings is to make holes in a wall; in this way, the opening is surrounded by the same type of structural fabric on all sides (78). The connection between the wall and the material in the opening (door or window frame or glass) is then more or less the same on all sides. An alternative approach is to make vertical slits in the wall or to enlarge the gap between neighbouring wall sections, thus creating an opening (80). In this case, the opening will be surrounded by surfaces (floor slabs, walls or roofs) of a different type and composition. The connection between the opening and the surrounding surfaces will therefore differ accordingly.

77

Openings in primary and complementary system.
The window lintels form part of the primary system accepting loads from the ceiling slabs.

78

Similar connections on all sides
The junctions with the opening are the same all around since one homogenous system is punctured.

79

Openings in the complementary system
Loads do not have to be redirected.

80

Different connections on all sides
Due to the system, a different junction of the opening is required on all four sides.

Vertical relations between spaces

Multiplication of space

The need to create multiple spaces on a limited area of ground has led builders to arrange spaces vertically above and below one another. A number of additional considerations now have to be borne in mind. Apart from the necessity to provide access to higher floors via a ramp, stairs or technical facilities such as a lift or escalator, the structure of the primary system will differ basically from that of a building where all spaces are arranged on the same level. In the first place, the load due to wind increases exponentially with height, partly because the wind pressure is greater at greater heights and partly because the bending moment increases squared to the height. In the second place, the structure of each storey has to bear the weight of all storeys above it. The designer will have to work out an appropriate strategy to deal with these problems. One solution is to make the loadbearing structure larger at lower levels in the building, as a result of which the enclosed spaces will become successively smaller (81). Alternatively, stronger materials can be used at lower level, thus keeping the dimensions of the loadbearing structure and the enclosed spaces the same. In concrete structures, for example, this can be achieved by using concrete with a higher compressive strength and/or more reinforcement, or steel structures in which the component steel sections have a higher web thickness (82, 83).

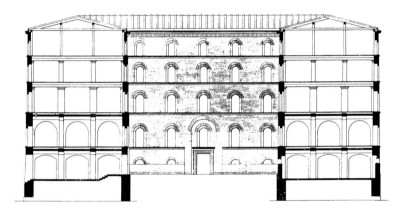

81

Neuer Packhof, Berlin, Karl Friedrich Schinkel, 1829
The construction of the lower storeys supports the loads of the upper storeys and is therefore dimensioned much larger.

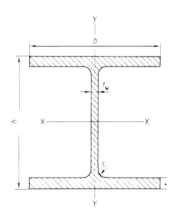

82

HEA steel profile
Loads are absorbed by a tension and a compression flange.

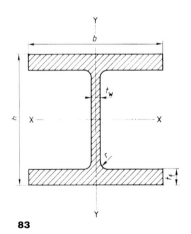

83

HEM steel profile
The external dimensions of the profiles are similar, but the HEM profile can accept higher loads due to the greater thickness of material.

Additive vertical multiplication of space

Within a unitary spatial module and its primary system, a smaller, largely independent space can be created. The added space does not contribute considerably to the strength, stiffness and stability of the structure as a whole but rather represents a load on the structure defining the larger space. The motivation for such a choice could be that the smaller space is of minor importance, that it might possibly be removed later or that it was added after the original construction phase. The designer may also have intended to give the impression that the smaller space is a subsidiary part of the higher and wider space. The wish to articulate the construction or the need to reflect the nature of the construction process in the external aspect of the building could also be a reason to choose such an approach.

An example of the application of this method is the Musée des Travaux Publics (1936–1937), designed by Auguste Perret (84). Heavy columns carry the roof which spans the entire depth of the building. A set of more closely spaced but lighter columns supports the mezzanine floor and is quite independent of the roof-bearing structure.

A similar approach is found in the government buildings that Michelangelo erected round the Campidoglio in Rome (85). Here, the tall columns extending over the whole height of the building appear to support the roof while free-standing round columns appear to carry the first floor and the parts of the façade supported by it.

A third example is the mezzanine in the library of Jo Coenen's Dutch Architectural Institute in Rotterdam from 1993. The mezzanine floors are suspended from the primary beams spanning the entire interior space (86).

85

Palazzo dei Conservatori, Rome, Michelangelo, 1563
The tall, continuous pilaster strips seem to support the roof while free-standing round columns support the top floor.

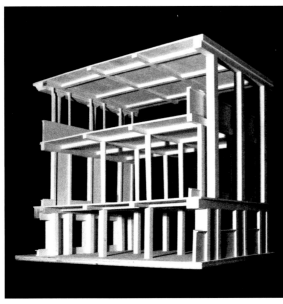

84

Musée des Travaux Publics, Paris, Auguste Perret, 1946
The columns of the bottom floors are independent of the roof columns.

86

Library of the Dutch Architectural Institute, Rotterdam, Jo Coenen, 1993
The gallery is suspended from the primary structure via tensioned rods.

Integral vertical multiplication of space

Here the spaces are stacked one on top of the other. Each layer has to bear the weight of the floor above it and the other structures resting on that. Once again, two options may be distinguished:

- The main loadbearing structure is the same on all storeys. Vertical loads are directly transmitted in a vertical direction to the foundations. The building method is the same for all storeys, and the stability problem is also solved in the same way on each storey.

- Alternatively, the main loadbearing structure can largely differ from the structure on individual storeys, which may possess a much broader or narrower grid. This approach permits the stacking of different building methods. The methods used to solve the stability problem will differ from storey to storey and between construction methods (87, 88).

87

Pavillon Suisse, Paris, Le Corbusier, 1933
The grid of columns on the top floors follows the required room dimensions. The ground level follows the conditions of the building's environment.

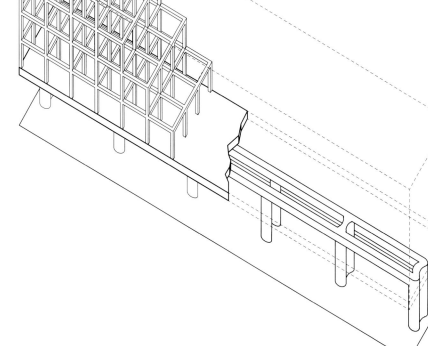

88

Pavillon Suisse, Paris, Le Corbusier, 1933
Axonometric view

Connection of space

Spaces located above or below of each other can be connected by means of stairs, a ramp, lift or escalator. The following comments about stairs apply equally to the other means of vertical access. A vital question is whether the stairs are to be situated inside or outside the space. The easiest method is to have the stairs outside (89, 90). In this case, the floor structure is not interrupted. This approach has the consequence, however, that one has to leave the building to get upstairs. This is not a problem in sunny, dry climates; hence, this method is widely used there. One way of making this approach climate-proof is to enclose the stairs in a separate two-storey stairwell (91, 92).

89

Residential building, Naxos, Greece
The external stair is located outside of the primary system.

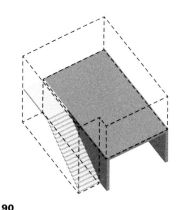

90

The external stair is located outside of the primary system
Schematic view

91

Sanatorium Zonnestraal, Hilversum, Netherlands, Johannes Duiker, 1928
The internal stair is located outside of the primary system.

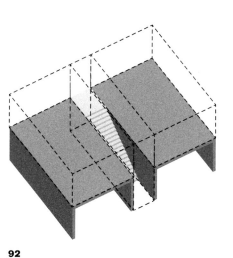

92

The internal stair is located outside of the primary system
Schematic view

The Richards Medical Research Laboratories (73) provide a good example of this. All stairwells and service ducts are situated outside the floor area of the laboratories.

In more complex buildings, we can arrange the individual spatial units around a stairwell to the upper storeys (93). The combined spaces then form an elegant structural unit, while the floor separating the spaces can partially project into the double-height stairwell to form a landing or half-landing.

This construction is often found in the stairwells of blocks of flats. The stairwell forms a separate spatial unit, whose walls support the landings as well as the floor slabs of the flats accessed by the stairs. These walls are part of the primary system. They have a separating and a loadbearing function.

When the stairs are situated within the spatial unit, the primary system – or at least part of it, that is: the upper floor slab – will have to be interrupted (94). Special structural measures will always have to be taken to deal with the interruption of the primary system.

Such measures are often found in connection with internal stairs in terraced houses. Since there are no loadbearing walls to support the floor where the stairs pass through it, a trimmer beam has to be provided for this purpose (95, 96).

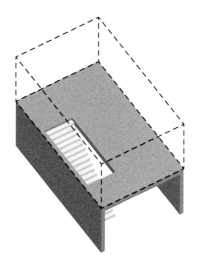

94

Stair integrated into primary system
Schematic view

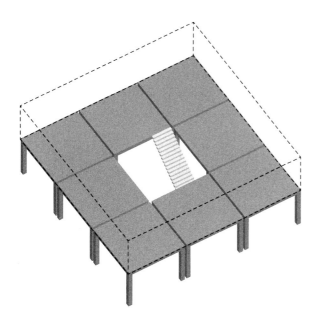

93

Internal stair in a void formed by the primary system
The stair opening is arranged by grouping the units around it.

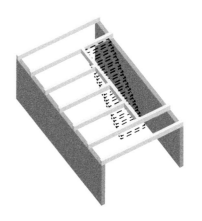

95

Stair opening crossing main span direction
Schematic view

It has been mentioned that any openings made in walls of the primary system should preferably be narrow. A relationship also exists between the structural function of the floor and the shape of any holes made in it. An opening represents an interruption of the structure. The floor surface transfers any loads on it to the ground in at least two opposite directions. This is no longer possible where an opening occurs. Hence, the load on the parts of the floor that have been cut away has to be dealt with by the neighbouring parts of the floor that are still left. They must be designed to make this possible. The more openings are made in a floor, the more problems arise in connection with the transfer of loads to the ground.

As mentioned before, the building methods described here are only models, basic spatial and structural constructs each with its own regularities and logic. Buildings are not copies of these models, and the author does not wish in any way to suggest that buildings that cannot be clearly classified under one of these types are not proper buildings. These models are not intended to serve as an ideal image supporting some kind of building standard, nor do they implicate a certain law or moral code with which building design should comply.

So what is their significance?

At a basic level, the building models described here establish a connection between spaces and the relationships between them on the one hand and materials and constructional methods on the other. Analysis of his own design and comparison with the models described will help the designer to take decisions about the shape and position of openings in space-defining structures, about stability and extendibility, about the nature of structures spanning space and the connections between the different parts of a building. It will be clear that considerations of utility and economy are also important here. There is no immutable law which states that floors in solid constructions must be supported all the way around, that rectangular stairwells can never be made at right angles to the main beams or that wide window openings can never be made in loadbearing walls or shells. These can be good solutions, but the designer should at least realise that they are not the ideal solutions from a structural point of view. If he or she chooses a more expensive design on technical or aesthetic grounds, this choice should be made after due consideration so that the extra complexity of the construction, and the impending extra building cost, will not come as a surprise but will already have been taken into account during the decision-making process.

96

Trimmer beams within a ceiling construction
The top of the stair is supported by a trimmer beam spanning two primary girders.

Authors

Ir. Maarten Meijs was trained as an architect and worked at practices in the Netherlands. Nowadays he is heading the educational staff in the chair of Professor Knaack, Delft University of Technology, Netherlands. He published on façades and other aspects of buildings, for instance the book *Cladding of Buildings* (with Alan Brookes).

Professor Dr. Ing. Ulrich Knaack is an architect and worked in an architectural practice in Düsseldorf. Today, he is Professor for Design of Construction and Building Technology at the Delft University of Technology, Netherlands; he is also Professor for Design and Construction at the University of Applied Sciences in Detmold, Germany. He is author of several well-known reference books on glass in architecture and editor of the publication series *Principles of Construction*.

Selected Bibliography

Alan Blanc
Internal Components (Mitchell's Building Series)
Longman, London, 1996

Alan Brookes, Maarten Meijs
Cladding of Buildings
Taylor and Francis, London, 4th edition 2008

Francis D.K. Ching
Building Construction Illustrated
John Wiley, New York, 3rd edition 2000

Jean-Nicolas-Louis Durand, Introduction:
Antoine Picon
Précis of the Lectures on Architecture:
With Graphic Portion of the Lectures
on Architecture
The Getty Research Institute, Los Angeles, 2000
(original edition Précis des leçons d'architecture
données à l'École Polytechnique, published
1802, 1805)

Edward R. Ford
The Details of Modern Architecture, vol. 1 and 2
MIT Press, Cambridge, Massachusetts, 1990
and 1996

Kenneth Frampton
Studies in Tectonic Culture
MIT Press, Cambridge, Massachusetts, 1995

Klaus-Peter Gast
Louis I. Kahn: The Idea of Order
Birkhäuser Verlag, Basel, 1998

Thomas Herzog, Roland Krippner, Werner Lang
Facade Construction Manual
Birkhäuser Verlag, Basel, and Edition Detail,
Munich, 2004

Ulrich Knaack, Tillmann Klein, Marcel Bilow,
Thomas Auer
Façades: Principles of Construction
Birkhäuser Verlag, Basel, 2007

Patrick Loughran
Failed Stone: Problems and Solutions with
Concrete and Masonry
Birkhäuser Verlag, Basel, 2006

Bruce Martin
Joints in Building
G. Godwin, London, and John Wiley and Sons,
New York, 1977

Michael McEvoy
External Components (Mitchell's Building Series)
Longman, London, 4th rev. edition, 1994

Andrea Palladio
The Four Books of Architecture
Dover, New York, 1965 (reprint MIT Press,
Cambridge, Massachusetts, 2001;
original edition Quattro libri dell'architettura,
Venice, 1570)

Ulrich Pfammatter
The Making of the Modern Architect and
Engineer: The Origins and Development of a
Scientific and Industrially Oriented Education
Birkhäuser Verlag, Basel, 2000

Heinz Ronner, Fredi Kölliker, Emil Rysler
Baustruktur: Baukonstruktion im Kontext
des architektonischen Entwerfens
Birkhäuser Verlag, Basel, 1995

Bjørn Normann Sandaker
On Span and Space: Exploring Structures
in Architecture
Taylor & Francis, London, 2007

Helmut C. Schulitz, Werner Sobek,
Karl J. Habermann
Steel Construction Manual
Birkhäuser Verlag, Basel, and Edition Detail,
Munich, 2000

Pete Silver, William McLean
Introduction to Architectural Technology
Laurence King Publishing, London, 2008

Michael Stacey
Component Design
Architectural Press, Oxford, 2001

Jan van der Woord
Gieten en kneden
Faculteit Bouwkunde, TU Delft, Delft, 2006

Osamu Wakita and Richard Linde
The Professional Practice of Architectural
Detailing
John Wiley and Sons, New York, 3rd edition,
1999

Klaus Zwerger
Wood and Wood Joints:
Building Traditions of Europe and Japan
Birkhäuser Verlag, Basel 1997

Index

Illustration Credits

Chapter 1

2 Foster & Partners
4 Ulrich Knaack

Chapter 2

7 Ulrich Knaack
30, 31 Engbert van der Zaag
35 Marcel Bilow

Chapter 3

4, 19 Alan Brookes
5 Ger van der Vlugt
35 Marcel Bilow
62 Unilin Nederland
68 From: Klaus Zwerger, *Wood and Wood Joints*, Birkhäuser Verlag, Basel, 1997
71 Ulrich Knaack
75 Simon Kenny

Chapter 4

1, 2, 4, 9, 10 , 25, 26, 27, 45, 46, 72, 76, 90, 92, 93, 94, 95 TU Delft, based on drawings by Heinz Ronner
7 Engbert van der Zaag
11 Jan van de Voort
12 Linda Hildebrand
13, 30 © 1973 Lloyd Kahn. From: Shelter, Shelter Publications, Bolinas, 1973
15 From: Andrea Palladio, *The Four Books of Architecture*, Dover Publications, New York, 1965
16 Alistair Hunter
17, 18 From: Colin Davies, *The Work of Michael Hopkins and Partners*, Phaidon, London, 1993
19, 20 Klaus-Peter Gast
22, 24 Photographs: Kim Zwarts. Courtesy of Barragán Foundation, Birsfelden, Switzerland
23 Wim van den Bergh (drawing of floor plan)
28 Enrico Cano
33 From: Walter Muir Whitehill, *Spanish Romanesque Architecture of the Eleventh Century*, Oxford University Press, London, 1941
34, 37, 58 Foster & Partners
35 Ken Kirkwood
36 Alan Howard
40 Drawing based on information by Renzo Piano
41 From: Yukio Futagawa, Niklaus Morgenthaler, *Atelier 5*, ADA Edita, Tokyo, 1976
42, 44 Atelier 5, Bern
47 Tim Street Porter
49 From: *Architecture* (Indonesian Heritage Series), Archipelago Press, Singapore, 1990
50, 51, 53 Reinhardt Blunck
52 Glenn Murcutt
55, 56, 57 Thomas Herzog
58, 59 Richard Davies
60 Foster & Partners
62, 63 Ezra Stoller © Esto
64 TU Delft
73, 81, 84, 88 MIT Press
75 Joop van Stigt
86 Ulrich Knaack

All other drawings were generated by the TU Delft; all other photographs are by Maarten Meijs.

We are especially grateful to these image providers. Every reasonable attempt has been made to identify owners of copyright.
Should unintentional mistakes or omissions have occurred, we sincerely apologise and ask for notice. Such mistakes will be corrected in the next edition of this publication.

Façades
Principles of Construction
Ulrich Knaack, Tillmann Klein, Marcel Bilow, Thomas Auer
135 pp. 305 ills. Softcover
ISBN 978-3-7643-7962-9

Prefabricated Systems
Principles of Construction
Ulrich Knaack, Sharon Chung-Klatte, Reinhard Hasselbach
136 pp. 280 ills. Softcover
ISBN 978-3-7643-8747-1
July 2009

Birkhäuser Verlag AG
Postfach 133
CH-4051 Basel

Tel. +41 61 205 07 07
e-mail: sales@birkhauser.ch
www.birkhauser.ch